Striking & Fielding Games

John Severs

STANLEY THORNES

Acknowledgements

The author would like to acknowledge the help given by Ruth Chilton, Jos Faulder, Jane Kelly, Karen Levitt, David Lowe, Ruth Rigby and Will Smiles with three of the activities in the book; and to thank pupils from Birtley East Primary School (Gateshead LEA) and King James 1st Secondary School, Bishop Auckland (Durham LEA) for their help with the illustrations.

©John Severs 1994

All rights reserved

First published in the United Kingdom by
Simon & Schuster Education
This edition published by Stanley Thornes (Publishers) Ltd,
Ellenborough House, Wellington Street, Cheltenham GL50 1YW
96 97 98 99 00/10 9 8 7 6 5 4 3 2 1

No part of this publication may be reproduced, stored in a retrieval system, or transmitted in any form or by any means, electronic, mechanical, photocopying, recording or otherwise, without prior permission of the publisher.

A catalogue record of this book is available from the British Library

ISBN 07487 2934 8

Printed in the United Kingdom by
Ashford Colour Press Ltd, Gosport, Hants

Contents

Introduction

Unit 1	Principles of play	3
Unit 2	Practices for fielding, bowling and batting	10
Unit 3	Rounders-type games	27
Unit 4	Cricket-type games	46
Unit 5	Longball, softball, stoolball and minor games	55
Unit 6	Making up practices and games	69
Unit 7	Lesson form, organisation and safety	72
Unit 8	Development and assessment	80
Appendix 1	Useful sources of information	88
Appendix 2	Dimensions and equipment sizes	89
Appendix 3	Proficiency awards	91

Introduction

This book is intended for all primary teachers and secondary school PE specialists who are concerned with satisfying the demands of the National Curriculum in Games at Key Stages 2 and 3. It is also intended for students who are covering curriculum or specialist courses.

Both the simple basic throwing, catching, rolling, batting and bowling practices which should be fully covered in the latter part of Key Stage 1 and the early part of Key Stage 2, and descriptions of techniques, are covered more than adequately in other publications (*see Appendix 1*). This book, therefore, concentrates on showing how opportunities can best be given for pupils to

- improve a range of skills, some specialist, and, as stated in the National Curriculum, 'refine and adapt' them in different game situations
- experience different roles within the games, including officiating
- learn to evaluate the results of different experiences and suggest ways of effecting improvement
- be 'physically active' throughout much of the lesson time.

This is largely achieved by doing the following:

1 Providing a range of fielding, batting and bowling practices, separately and combined, with many replicating actual game situations and involving competition and scoring.

2 Covering a very wide range of different types of striking/ fielding games
   - using different types of balls and other objects, projected in a variety of ways
   - matched to the different achievement levels and needs of the pupils working on Key Stages 2 and 3.

Many well-known and less well-known team games are covered, including a great many based on rounders' principles and different forms of cricket, with a few even combined with skills such as kicking or different types of dribbling, which are more normally associated with 'invasion' games.

3 Structuring activities to allow
   - batters equal opportunities and
   - in many cases, the majority, if not all, of the fielders to play an active part when each hit is made.

4 Advocating 'solo' versions of games, in which everyone is always involved, and in which all players, through rotation, may experience all types of role.

5 Stressing the use of small-side team games, some scaled down from major versions (the value of activity of this sort is stressed in the National Curriculum Programmes of Study for both Key Stages 2 and 3).

6 Devoting a section to the making-up of practices or games in groups, activity which, providing the right foundation has been laid, can be both rewarding and valuable in respect of understanding the functioning of games, the need for rules, etc and which, again, fulfils a particular need as stressed in the National Curriculum.

7 Including crucial back-up sections on

   a how to organise the content, using pairs, small groups, etc, working in parallel at different activities, so that material can be matched to each child's needs

   b development and assessment, which outlines in some detail how both class and individual progress in skill and understanding can be planned and monitored – this has particular value in that the National Curriculum states that teachers should set up their own modes

   c how to set up games and practices safely.

Additionally, as suggested in the National Curriculum, some stress is laid on showing how children may

- learn to understand the nature of the roles played
- appreciate the nature of and reasons for rules
- begin to appreciate strengths and weaknesses of individuals, including self, in different roles and align this to the ability to solve problems and/or use strategies in practices and games of all kinds, eg in the making-up of games when problems occur.

Finally, the book includes diagrams, with measurements where necessary for standardised courts, and appendices giving useful sources of information, information on recommended dimensions and equipment sizes to correspond to different ages and/or sexes, and information on proficiency awards.

Unit 1 *Principles of play*

Traditional summer field games, particularly cricket and rounders, have been played in British schools for many decades and continue to be enjoyed to varying degrees by many children.

However, while not denying the need to experience the full game, critics have pointed out that given

- the limitations in time available
- the need, as stressed in the National Curriculum, for all pupils to experience plenty of activity, and
- the further need for reasonably equal opportunity for all,

these games played in their traditional form week in and week out may not be serving the best interests of the pupils.

They claim that what the pupils actually need throughout Key Stages 2 and 3 is step-by-step development matched to actual progress, with a stress on graded **practices** and types of game that allow maximum participation and opportunities for **all** to improve the full range of skills involved.

Pupils should

- learn the basic techniques involved in batting, bowling and fielding
- apply them as soon as possible, as skills in game-related – and possibly competitive – practices
- develop them in actual games, some with small sides and others, often strongly related to 'the real thing', that are structured to allow all to score, stress certain skills, etc
- finally, but possibly to a limited degree, experience the full game.

As already stated, this book concentrates on more advanced technique and game-associated practices and a large variety of games, many designed or structured to allow for more equal participation.

The format and rules employed in the modified or alternative game versions ensure that

- those in 'fielding' situations are much more active than in standard versions
- when batting, all have equal opportunities in terms of the number of balls received
- all may have in-built opportunities to practise bowling skills

- all players have an active role throughout the game.

It is essential that no pupil spends long periods simply watching others making high scores. Poorer players tend to be out quite soon in both cricket and rounders, and may suffer long periods of inactivity – and possibly alienation from the game. If the full game is played all the time, such pupils do not get proper opportunity to redress their weaknesses.

Many of the games can be played with small sides, as is advocated in the National Curriculum. This not only allows for matching of ability but also gives more direct opportunity for batting, bowling and fielding, and is of particular value in Key Stage 2.

Cricket-type games

Cricket games, some promoted by the National Cricket Association (*see Appendix 1*), have been devised which allow for **all** participants to gain adequate practice and therefore improve. The basis for these games is, normally,

- a big reduction in the total numbers taking part in the game
- small sides, even as low as just a pair, competing as batting units
- equal opportunity for all players to experience batting, bowling and fielding
- through repeated innings, the opportunity to take up specialist fielding positions (eg wicket-keeper).

A typical format applying to some of the games and scoring practices would include

- all players receiving a set number of balls
- all starting with a base individual score of, say, 10 or 100
- when 'out', to a catch for example, batters continue to occupy the crease but lose, say, from three to six runs from the total scored.

In some cases a game may be based on sets of pairs working on a rota basis with one unit batting, one bowling and the others fielding. No player ever 'sits out' when dismissed or when waiting for a turn, as happens in the full game (*see Solo (or Pairs) rota games below*).

More rarely a 'ceiling' is imposed, with batters retiring when reaching a previously set score. When this rule is established, players readily accept it and get great satisfaction in reaching a target and being 'not out'.

Principles of play

Rounders-type games

In rounders the game structure works heavily against poorer players. This is because

- they are often weaker hitters and/or runners and are therefore out more quickly
- they have to watch the harder and/or more accurate hitters and stronger runners enjoying more turns and scoring many more rounders
- they are often poorer at catching and throwing long distances and thus take less part or gain less satisfaction in the field.

It is possible, however, to play a whole variety of rounders-related games for much of the time, which are designed so that

- all can make a positive contribution to the game
- all the games retain the basic principle of hitting, or propelling forwards in some other way, a ball or other object, and running round a number of bases
- because of the different nature of what the players may be required to do, a particular game may be selected as being ideally suited to a given point in ability development within a particular Key Stage.

The system works as follows:

1. Five or six markers are spaced out, possibly in a rough semicircle (for outside or a sports hall) or a rectangle (in a restricted rectangular space such as a gym – *see diagrams, pages 5 and 6*).

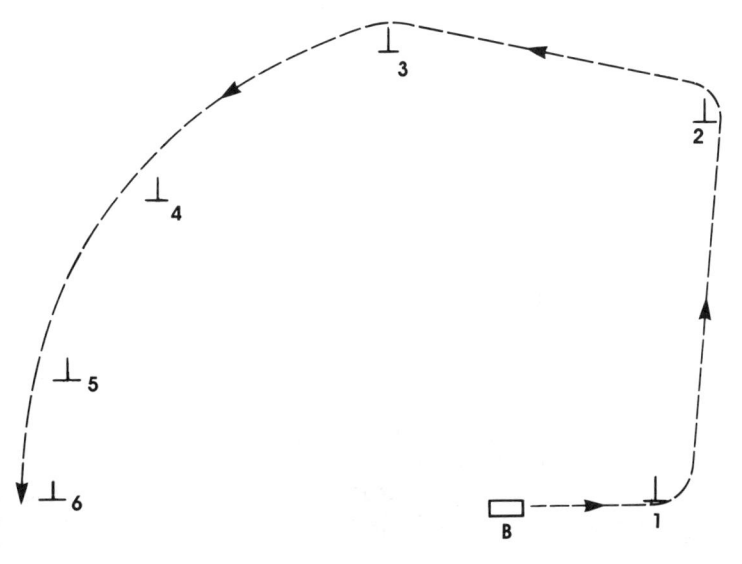

B = Batting base

5

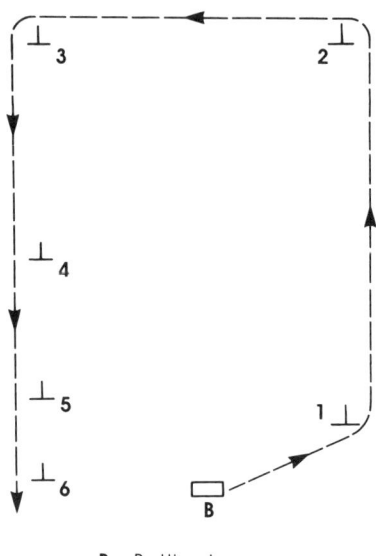

Striking and Fielding Games

B = Batting base

2 The distance from the batting point to the first base is kept short.

3 Ideally, the distances between bases decrease with each successive marker after base **2** (ie with base **1** to base **2** the longest), but this is not essential.

4 Both the inter-base measures and the total distance round all the bases must be flexible and can be changed in respect of
- different ability levels
- the numbers playing
- the actual game being played and the rules employed and
- particularly, what happens in practice.

Therefore, unlike the game of rounders itself, the marker positions are not fixed.

5 Each child has just one turn per innings.

6 He/she aims to forward hit, kick, etc an object such as a ball, and attempts to run past as many bases as possible before the fielders complete a given task.

The **task** could be based on the following:

- Up to six fielders roll or throw a ball from person to person.

- When a fielder has taken a catch and thrown the ball on, he/she sits down (or crouches if it is damp) to show that they are now 'out of the game', thus ensuring that, say, six different children handle the ball.

- If attempted catches are dropped then they **may** be deemed not to count and other players may be involved in order to achieve the required number of catches. If, however, quite a number of children are still prone to drop the ball, it may be accepted that the fielding team has been 'punished' sufficiently through the loss of time taken in retrieving the ball, and extra catches will not be required.

7 A player's individual score is the number of bases that he or she passes.

8 Individual scores are added to give the team score.

As stated, the inter-base distances are geared to the game and the number of fielders involved in the task. They should be selected to ensure that

- all players score at least one point (this is why it is important to keep the distance from the striking point to the first base short – although in most cases the nature of the task would ensure that this point is reached comfortably, regardless of the length)
- most players score in the middle range, ie three or four points
- the maximum number of points possible (ie passing the last base) is attainable but difficult.

The benefits of this excellent system are that

- all players are able to score on each batting turn
- although 'better' hitters/stronger runners may on average score more points, players with less ability can occasionally score highly
- poorer players can sometimes contribute the vital winning points (more than once the situation has been observed where the final member of the team batting last required, say, three points to win the game and just achieved it – or just failed, thus achieving an exciting draw)
- no player has more chances than any other player, and
- more fielders are active on each batter's turn with, in some instances, all taking part in the task.

Alternatively it is possible to give batters the opportunity to score an unlimited number of runs. This is done by allowing them to attempt a second circuit of the markers if the fielders have not finished the task when the last base is passed. It would appear in practice, however, that most pupils are happy to finish with a set maximum, and sense that over-large scores detract from the game.

There is one situation, though, where allowing this to happen, on occasion, is recommended. When the final batter for the

Striking and Fielding Games

team batting last (ideally in this situation one of the stronger players) comes in and his/her team's total at that point is more than five points behind their opponents' completed total, thus making it impossible for that team to win on normal scoring, it is possible to revive interest markedly by allowing unlimited scoring **on that turn only.**

Solo (or Pairs) rota games

Most of the rounders, the stoolball, and some of the cricket-type games can be organised so that they take place on a 'solo' basis. This operates as follows:

1 A group of, say, eight to ten work together.

2 One player bats and the remainder act as the fielding side.

3 When the first striker has had an 'innings', he/she joins the fielders and another player takes over.

4 An innings normally consists of, in rounders, from one to three good balls and, in cricket, one or two six-ball overs.

5 Scores can be cumulative over successive innings.

The game is thus organised on an individual competition basis.

It may also be based on what is termed a 'rota' system where, when a striker has received a given number of balls, everyone changes round: say bowler to batter, batter to backstop/wicket-keeper, backstop or wicket-keeper to base/fielder, and so on.

- This is useful when a class or games group is too big to be split into just two teams for a given game but not big enough to create four teams for two games.

- The class can be split into three equal sets (of, say, 10–12) with two sets playing each other at the main game, and the other group playing a solo rota version of either the same or a different game.

- When both teams playing the game have had an innings each, the solo group plays one of these teams, with the remaining team playing the solo game.

An attractive alternative is for the players to operate in pairs.

In rounders
- Each pair member may bowl to the other, thus helping to produce 'fair' balls.

- The remaining pairs act as fielders.

- Scores are added to give a pair's team total.

In cricket-type games
Where batters operate as normal, with sets of wickets at each end of the pitch (as opposed to the solo version where there is just one set of stumps), rota games must operate on a pairs basis.

This also applies in stoolball.

These systems, although not always as immediately attractive to some children as a full team game, have the big advantage of giving everyone an active role.

Game-related practices

Such practices, normally played in small groups of 3–6, allow a skill such as a batting shot in cricket, a hit in rounders, or a pick-up and return, to be developed under the same sort of conditions as would be experienced in a game. For example:

- Fielding returns to balls that have been hit, thrown or rolled with some accuracy are matched in some way to one or more runners negotiating one or more bases or wickets.

- In having to hit the ball into a given area, or use a certain type of shot/hit, etc to a ball bowled in a prescribed way, a batter is able to score, and can be out in a variety of ways (normally losing runs and staying in for a set number of balls, with sets possibly repeated), thus experiencing the same pressures as in a game. Given the small numbers involved, with so many more turns guaranteed, repeated practice at a particular facet of a skill is possible.

- Motivation is good and confidence can be built through working with other pupils of similar ability.

Hopefully such skills can be developed in these helpful conditions to the point where they can be more readily sustained through the more demanding small side and solo game situations until, eventually, the full game can be played with some expectation of success.

Practices and games played under such conditions, matched to ability levels and needs, often based on smaller numbers than the 'full' version and allowing increased opportunity for the majority to make improvements, are exactly what is required in satisfying the demands of the National Curriculum at Key Stages 2 and 3.

Unit 2 *Practices for fielding, bowling and batting*

Much properly structured practice is needed at each Key Stage in order for all pupils to develop the skills needed to play summer field games well. The skills associated with these games embrace

- fielding, including
  - catching and taking bounces
  - picking up from the ground
  - returning via throwing, rolling, etc
- hitting/batting, etc
- bowling
- running
- those associated with understanding the game, including tactics.

This unit concentrates on the more demanding skills practices, many competitive, which have obvious links to the game and which in some cases are suited to the latter part of Key Stage 2 and, in others, to the more advanced Key Stage 3.

Two particular points should be stressed, however:

1 All pupils should follow through a process, starting with the very simple practices such as throwing and catching a beanbag or rolling a ball at close range in Key Stage 1, and finally moving on to those practices that replicate game elements in pressure situations.

2 This basic work is essential and must be completed before more advanced practices can be attempted – if necessary continuing into the secondary school (year 7) in order to do so.

Fielding practices

Medium to long distance

Distances can be increased with practice. A good basic distance to start with could be that between rounders bases, ie 12 metres.

Working in pairs

a Basic throwing and catching, the ball being thrown quite high.

Practices for fielding, bowling and batting

b As for **a** but aiming for a fast, hard throw direct to the chest.

c One player, **A**, aims to keep one or both feet in a small hoop or stands behind springed stumps or two large skittles. The other player, **B**, fed bounced balls by **A**, throws in hard from different distances.

d Both players aim to keep their feet in hoops – fast, hard throws.

e Aim to bounce the ball in a hoop placed in front of the receiver.

f The ball is placed on the ground alongside the feet – aim to pick up, one step forward, fast, hard throw.

g **B** moves forward to pick up a dead ball using the recommended side-on shuffle with the pick-up being made in the throwing position – aim to throw in one action from the ground direct to **A**.

h • **A** feeds a rolling ball towards **B** who, initially using the basic fielding position designed to stop the ball rolling through the legs, gathers the ball, stands up and returns the ball.
   • **B** progresses to advancing a few steps towards the ball, and picking up and returning it, initially in two phases, later in one continuous action.
   • A bobbling ball (a low rapid bounce like 'ducks and drakes') may also be fed to **B**.

i **B** stands 1–3 metres in front of **A**, with both facing the same direction (*see diagram*). **A** rolls or gently lobs a ball past **B** who on seeing it only as it passes (he/she must **not** look behind or anticipate), chases after it, retrieves it, turns and returns it to **A** as soon as possible.

Striking and Fielding Games

j
- **A** throws for one bounce, rolls or bobbles the ball at different distances and angles.
- **B** moves across, picks up the ball cleanly and returns it as quickly as possible to **A**, standing behind a set of stumps, with one foot in a hoop or touching a rounders base.

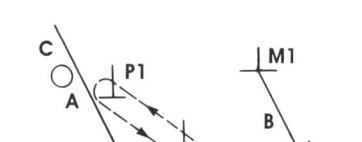

Working in threes

a
- **A** rolls the ball out towards the boundary.
- **B** picks it up and makes a long-distance return.
- **C** takes the ball on the bounce and returns it rapidly to **A** using an underhand or side-arm throw.

b
- **A** aims to 'beat' **B** by rolling or bouncing the ball over an imaginary or marked line between the markers **M**.
- Both the distance between the markers and that from them to **A**'s base line and/or hoop can be varied to match ability.
- If the ball crosses the line, **A** scores four points (or a boundary).
- If **B** picks up the ball, it is thrown immediately to **C** who is either behind the base line or ready to step into the hoop (whichever is being used).
- While the fielders return the ball, **A** aims to run as many times as possible round two posts or skittles **P**.
- The posts are placed at such a distance that normally one or two or, at the most, three runs can be scored.

c **A**, **B** and **C** stand in a triangle 12, 20, 25 metres, etc apart with, in each case, one foot on a base or in a hoop.
- The ball is thrown round the triangle.
- Each player after catching is required to move the feet through a 60° arc and into the correct position before throwing to the next in order.
- The order of throwing can be reversed.

These practices can be made into competitions.

- The class is split into threes (or with some fours to match total numbers), who stand equal distances apart and compete to be the first to make, say, 12 successful catches (*see Unit 6*).

- A better alternative is *Beat the record*, in which all groups aim to make as many successful catches as possible in a given time, say 20 or 30 seconds, and then repeat the process with the aim of improving their scores. Winners may also be declared, for achieving the highest score on each attempt.

For the competition to be meaningful it is essential that

- pupils know they **must** count the number of catches made, possibly calling out the running total as each catch is held
- all scores are checked after the first attempt
- in all competitions and practices the pupils follow the rules as set (eg in this case having a foot on the base or in the hoop when throwing on, and having to return to do this if the received ball has been thrown off line).

Otherwise the competition is pointless and the players will fail to develop the precision under pressure which is the object of the exercise.

If the pupils are following the rules and counting correctly, about two-thirds should improve on the second attempt. The same practice or competition can be based on rolling, underarm throwing, one bounce, one-handed catching, etc.

Working in fours (or more)

Calling catch

1. Three players, numbered, stand fairly close together.
2. A fourth player throws a ball towards them, from a minimum distance of 30 metres, sometimes high, sometimes on a lower parabola, and calls out the number of the player who must catch the ball. Difficulty can be increased by
   - altering the direction of the throw or dropping it a little short and therefore forcing the catchers to run further to take the ball
   - delaying the call so that quick reactions are needed to make the catch.

Bases catch

a Four players stand next to bases placed on or to replicate a rounders pitch.
   - A ball is thrown from player to player round the bases.
   - Contact is always made with the base before the ball is thrown on.

b *Catch and time*
   As for **a**, but
   - a complete 'circuit' is timed by a fifth player

- the process is repeated a number of times with the object of improving the time, all players taking turns as timer
- different modes of throwing may be tried to see if there are any differences in the times.

c *Catch and run*
- One player runs round the four posts continuously, touching each with a rounders stick and aiming to pass as many as possible as the basemen complete a set number of throws and catches (maintaining contact with or touching each base before each throw).
- All the players take turns at running round, the winner being the one who passes the most bases while the catches are being made.

This practice, played in ability groups, in developing the combined skills of throwing and catching with specific running for rounders and in allowing a lot of continuous activity, is an excellent example of what is required in satisfying the aims of the National Curriculum.

Target hitting

1. From four to six players make a square or circle round a set of stumps (springback on a metal base are ideal for this) or two skittles placed side by side.

2. Working from different distances and using underarm, side-on and overarm throws, one player aims to hit the wicket or skittles.

3. If successful another player attempts a hit. If not, one of the other players 'backs-up', possibly by running into position at the other side of the target, and in turn aims to hit. Two balls may be used at a more advanced stage, making all participants observe closely all the time.

Non-stop catching
Groups of four, five or six line up (*see diagram*).

1. Player **2** throws the ball quite high – shoulder height or above – to the side of player **3**, then runs behind player **5**.

2. Player **3** catches and throws (or rolls, bounces, etc according to distance/need, etc) the ball to player **1** and then immediately runs to take his/her place. Player **1** then takes **2**'s place and the process is repeated.

Short distance

In most of the following practices the distance can be varied with increases from a starting point of 3 to 5 metres up to 12 metres and beyond (ie moving into the middle-distance range) depending on the experience/age, etc of the pupils.

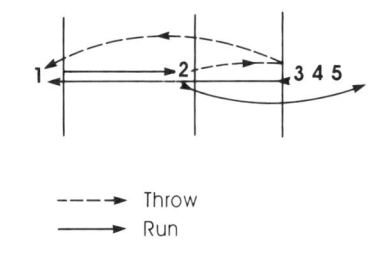

Practices for fielding, bowling and batting

Working in pairs

a The ball, lying dead on the ground a few metres from **B**, is flicked up to him/her by **A** using a strong wrist action.

b • The ball is rolled by **B** to the preferred hand side of **A** who can pounce on it and whip it in with a strong sideways action, or the ball is rolled straight to **A** who picks it up and quickly moves into the throwing position. Finally the ball is rolled towards the non-preferred hand side (normally weaker), of the player, who may
   • attempt the throw with the 'other' hand, or
   • collect and transfer to the preferred hand, or
   • run round the ball and use the preferred hand off the ground.

Speeds, angles and distances can be altered.

c As for **a** and **b**, but **B** stands behind a set of stumps or with one foot on a base, in a hoop, etc.

d The ball is thrown to a partner through distances of from 5 to 12 metres.

Static

The ball can be thrown, normally quite hard and fast, at different heights:

- low – aiming for the shins, the toes and in front of the feet so that one step forward must be taken
- high – so that a jump must be taken
- for one-handed catching, stressing a range of positions to each side of the body – say 2 o'clock to 5 on the left and 7 o'clock to 10 on the right – and gradually increasing the degree of stretch needed until a big sideways step with one foot is required.

Moving

The ball is thrown

- well short so that the catcher has to take some short sharp steps forward to reach it
- to the side so that two or three quick shuffling steps are needed – two- and one-handed catching should be practised

15

- high over the head – necessitating one or two steps backwards.

Always ensure that the practice is organised in such a way – in lines, for example – that there is no possibility of any pupils standing immediately behind the catchers.

Running

The ball is thrown into space – fairly hard – between head and knee height so that a full running movement is required in order to reach the ball. The angle or distance the catcher has to move through starts at a minimum level and is increased with success.

Working in threes

Player **A** rolls or bobbles the ball at right-angles or on a diagonal to **B** who runs in, picks it up with one hand or both hands and throws 'in' immediately to **C** who may/may not be stationed at a base, stumps, etc.

Working in fours (or more)

Pepper pot

1 Player **A** rolls or, more usually, throws a ball, initially in order and then randomly, to **B**, **C** and **D** at distances of, say, 4, 7 and 10 metres.

2 Each returns the ball to **A**.

3 When the players are competent, two balls may be introduced with the first ball only thrown back when the second is released by **A**, etc.

With younger players, **B**, **C** and **D** may call out immediately before throwing as a warning signal as to where the ball is coming from and when.

Beat the line

1 Four or five players defend a marked stretch of line (*see diagram*).

2 **A** and **B**, positioned 10 metres away, aim to breach the 'line' by rolling, bouncing or, possibly, throwing the ball through the gaps.

French hand cricket

1 One player **A** stands in a circle (minimum diameter 3 metres).

2 The other three to five players, outside the circle, aim to bounce or roll the ball so that it hits the target's legs (normally below the knee).

3 **A** either defends with one nominated hand, or attempts to catch or pick up the ball.

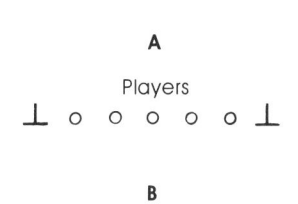

4 The throwers may never move with the ball in hand but in some versions are allowed to pass it to another player in a better attacking position.

Hand hockey

- Two teams of three or four aim to pass the ball from player to player by rolling or bouncing it below knee height. The object is to roll it into the opponent's goal.

- Teams may be increased by one if a designated goalkeeper is used as the only player allowed in a restricted 'D' in front of the goal.

- Skittles can be used as goal posts, with the distance between them matched to ability.

- The game may also be played using direct throwing below either shoulder or waist height in passing but not in scoring, in addition to or as an alternative to rolling, etc.

Relays

Shuttle rolling

1 Three players take up positions (*see diagram*). **A** is stationed, say, 10 metres away, and rolls a ball to **B**, then immediately runs to take up the position presently occupied by **B**.

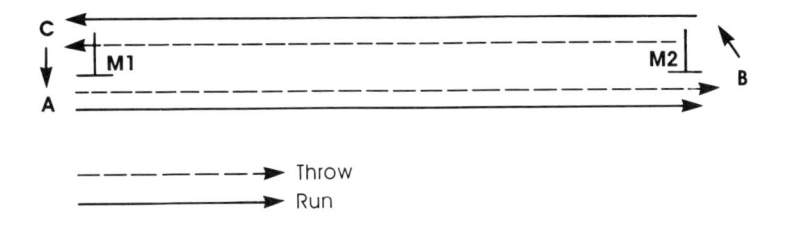

```
C ←─────────────────────────────
  ↓  ┌──┐                          ┌──┐  ↖
     │M1│ - - - - - - - - - - - -  │M2│    B
A ───┴──┴─────────────────────────┴──┴──→

- - - - - →  Throw
──────────→  Run
```

2 **B** picks up the ball, moves to the other side of marker **M1**, rolls the ball to **C** and runs to take **C**'s position.

3 Player **C**, in turn, picks up the ball, moves to the other side of marker **M2**, rolls the ball to **A** who is now in position behind line **L1** to the left of **M1**, runs, etc. The rolling thus becomes continuous and the winning team is the first to complete a set number of rolls and either sit down, crouch or raise hands, etc.

The reason for moving from one side of a marker to the other after receiving the ball is to stop players advancing towards the ball and cutting down the throwing/running distance.

Shuttle catching

- As for *Shuttle rolling*, but the ball is thrown.

- Five players may take part, three at the starting end, two at the other, to ensure full continuity.

Striking and Fielding Games

Tunnel rolling

1. Four players stand in line at equal intervals.

2. Player **A**, standing behind a line or at a marker, aims to roll a ball between **B** and **C**'s legs to **D** who is also behind a line or at a marker.

3. **D** picks up the ball, **B** and **C** turn round and **D** aims to roll the ball back through to **A**.

B and **C** only touch the ball if it moves out of line, stops short, etc. The competition may involve just two rolls or any multiple of two, and is normally repeated at least once with **B** and **C** changing places with **A** and **D**.

Catching and running
Two teams of four compete (*see Unit 7*).

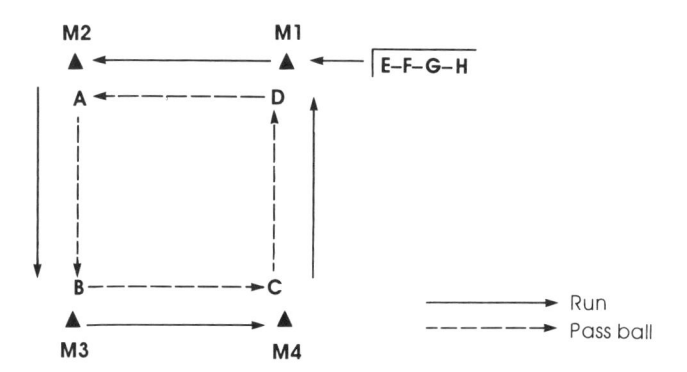

1. Team **1** – **A**, **B**, **C** and **D** – each stand with one foot in a hoop placed in a square formation, rounders base distance apart (12 metres).

2. Team **1** aims to make as many catches as possible, throwing the ball round the square in order, while team **2** (**E**, **F**, **G** and **H**) run, one at a time, round the markers **M1–4**.

Practices for fielding, bowling and batting

3 On completing a circuit, each runner either touches the next runner, or passes on (never throws) a baton, ball or quoit.

4 The teams then change places, with team **2** aiming to beat team **1**'s score.

It is vital that traditional relays or practices of the six or more in a team type, with each throwing and catching in turn with one at the front, are avoided, because
- the children, waiting turns, are not involved for most of the time
- the best form of basic throw and catch relays are based on continuous throwing in teams of three or four.

Running – first base home
This excellent fielding/running scoring practice can be made into a game. The practice/game is played on a rounders or modified pitch or softball diamond.

1 One player rolls or throws a ball below waist or head height into the field between first and third base from the batting base.

2 He/she then aims to reach first base before the fielders can retrieve the ball and throw it to the first base catcher.
- The practice can involve groups of **six**, with one player having several 'goes' at rolling/running before all rotate positions.
- The game could involve teams of **five**, with each player having one attempt in each innings, scoring one point if successful.

Bowling practices

Rounders, stoolball, longball

In pairs

a **A** and **B** stand 8 to 10 metres from each side of two posts and bowl the ball between two attached canes or, possibly, ropes. The canes, etc are fixed in parallel at points corresponding to the average knee and shoulder heights of the group taking part.

b **A** and **B** stand 16 to 20 metres apart with a medium- and, later, a small-sized hoop at the mid-point between them. They aim to bowl the ball to each other so that it passes over the hoop.

c Practices **a** and **b** can be combined. Both incorporate back-stop practice as well as bowling.

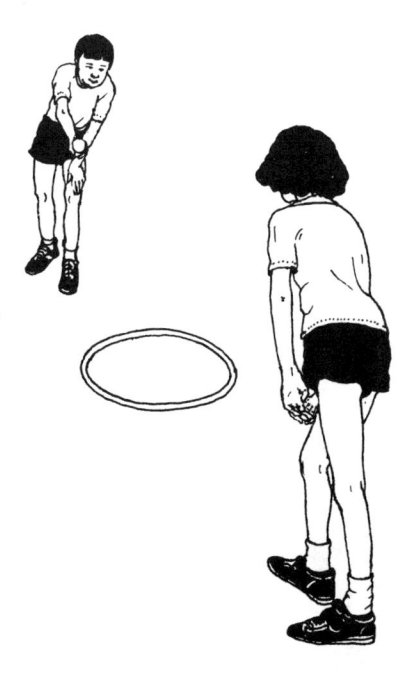

Striking and Fielding Games

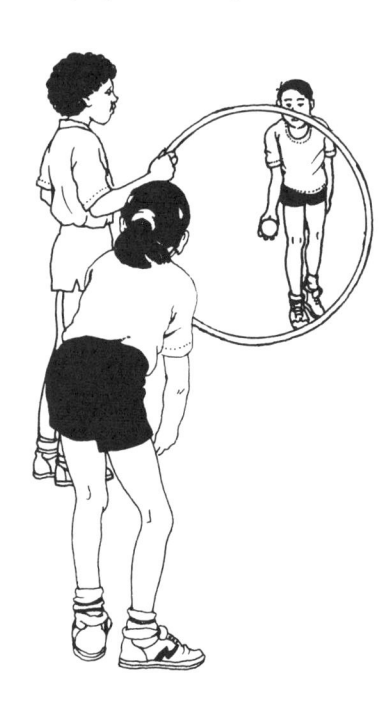

In threes

a **A** and **B** stand 16 metres apart
  - The ball is bowled through a hoop held vertically by **C** at the mid-point between them.
  - Large hoops should be used initially with size decreasing as accuracy improves.

b **B** adopts a normal back-stop position behind a batting square or hoop.
  - **A** bowls over the square/hoop and **B** immediately on receiving the ball throws it hard to **C** who is at first base on the rounders pitch or at a post placed at the equivalent point.
  - **C** returns the ball to **A**.
  - The classic 'missed-hit' situation in the game is thus replicated.

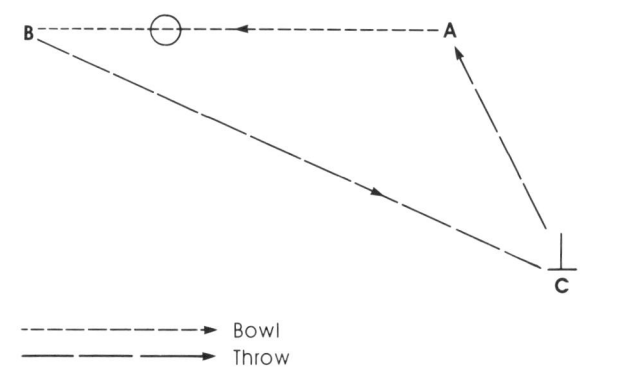

```
----------> Bowl
----------> Throw
```

Other bowling practices are combined with batting work.

Cricket

In pairs

a Basic technique can be developed through placing two large or medium hoops at a good distance apart (say 14–19 metres, depending on age).
  - **A** and **B** bowl alternately from each end.
  - They run up alongside one hoop and aim to pitch the ball so that it bounces in the other with each acting as 'wicket-keeper' to the other's bowling.

b Progression from **a** would necessitate using a set of stumps or skittles.
  - The ball is aimed at ground targets placed in front or to the off and leg sides of the stumps, etc.
  - The target may be an area marked with whitewash, a piece of canvas or strong card (nailed to the ground if possible), or a box or circle defined by skipping ropes or a hoop. Target size is adjusted to ability.

Practices for fielding, bowling and batting

Further developing and refining of technique may take place in nets, in practices combined with batting, where the length can be adjusted to the batter's reach, and in actual games.

Batting practices

Rounders

A flat padder bat should be used initially, with a tennis or rubber ball. Development should be towards bats designed for particular games, then harder balls.

As the object is to avoid the bowler by hitting the ball past or over her/him, it is necessary to use a fielder or fielders from the outset. If these practices are used at an early stage of learning and the batters miss the ball at times, a backstop will also be needed.

In threes (or fours)

Target hitting

a Batter **A** stands at the side of the square or hoop that the ball passes over.
  - The ball is bowled by **B** at the normal distance for a given game.
  - **A** aims to hit the ball downwards so that it passes either to the left or right of **B** and is then fielded and returned by **C**.

Greater accuracy is demanded by aiming to hit the ball so that it

- lands between marked lines or ropes laid out at intervals or in the vicinity of spaced out hoops, or
- is directed to pass between or over two markers positioned ahead (eg first and third base on a rounders pitch) or to one side.

b This practice can be made competitive by using the layout as shown in the diagram below.

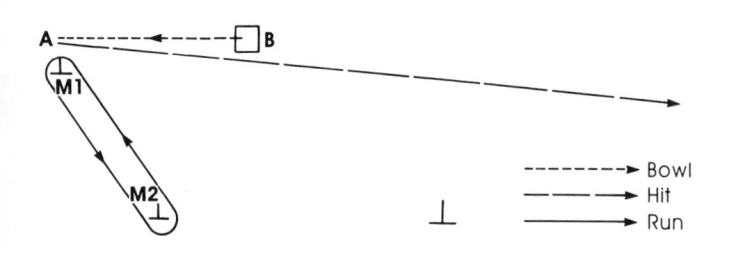

21

Striking and Fielding Games

- In order to score, **A** must hit the ball so that its path lies between the two bases, which are positioned according to ability.
- If successful, **A** attempts to run round the markers **M** as many times as possible before the ball is returned to **B**.
- If the ball is caught or returned to **B** in the bowling box or hoop while **A** is between markers, **A** scores nothing.
- Each player has six balls before changing round.
- When the hitting is strong, more than one fielder may be used.

See the following pages for batting practices that can be used for both rounders and cricket.

Cricket

Basic techniques should be learned with a 'bowler' standing about 5 metres from a batter and feeding balls as required, using either an underarm lob (eg for forward defence and drives) or an overarm 'push' with a high arm action to get the ball to bounce up to the appropriate height (eg for back defence, cuts).

In the case of defensive shots the practice is done in twos with the ball picked up by the feeder; for attacking shots where a fielder is required, in threes. (The illustration shows the position for practising a square cut.)

Further development can take place in nets, in the competitive practices described below, and in actual games of different types (*see Unit 4*).

Scoring practices suitable for rounders, softball and cricket

Hit the gap

1. Four posts are placed in line (*see diagram*). The gaps depend on the game skill being practised and the skill level expected, both in turn being linked to the distance from the striker (eg 10-metre gaps at 25 metres distance for cricket, 7-metre gaps at 15 metres for rounders).

2. If the ball is hit through (or possibly above in rounders and for some cricket shots) the middle gap between posts 2 and 3, two points are scored, and if through either of the other two, ie **1** to **2** and **3** to **4**, one point is scored.

3. Each batter receives six good balls (that is, one that is deliberately aimed to allow a given type of shot/strike to be made) at each turn, with a possible maximum of twelve points.

4. The posts are positioned to encourage or force a particular kind of shot in cricket or strike in rounders, etc. In the diagram, for example, the posts are placed for an off-drive in cricket, or a hit to the left of the bowler in rounders.

The posts could be positioned for different types of strike in rounders and shots in cricket where hitting the ball square (ie at right-angles to the stumps) or behind the wicket as well as in front can be encouraged, eg straight, leg, off and cover drives, pulls and cuts.

Beat the field

This practice for three or four players encourages accuracy, control and power in hitting, plus competent fielding.

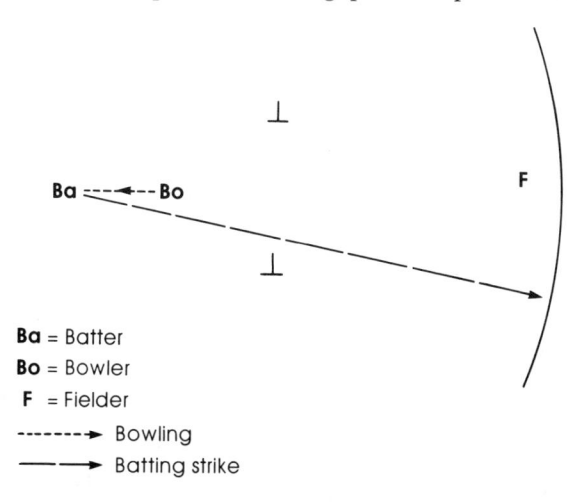

Ba = Batter
Bo = Bowler
F = Fielder
-------> Bowling
——→ Batting strike

1. The batter receives six good balls (underhand and overpitched in cricket, normal in rounders).

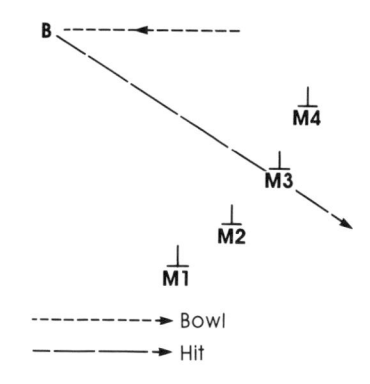

Striking and Fielding Games

2 He/she aims to hit/drive the ball
   - between the two markers
   - to beat both the bowler who is central and close, and the outfielder who is 'defending' the line or space beyond the markers.

3 The batter scores one point for hitting the ball between the markers, one point for beating the bowler, and one point for beating the fielder(s) who may have to stay within a given distance of the markers or defend an arc, say part of a boundary line.

4 The batter may lose one or an increasing number of points each time the ball is caught.

5 Depending on the distance between the markers and the power of the hitting, two outfielders may be used.

6 All players rotate after the six balls, and there may be repeated 'innings'.

Emphasis may be placed on hitting the ball along the ground, high in the air, or a mixture of both.

Hit the gap and *Beat the field* can be combined, with the arc being placed centrally or to the off or leg sides.

- The batter scores more points for hitting the ball accurately through the middle gap than for the two outer ones, and much higher if the fielder is beaten.

- Alternatively the fielder(s) may stand in front of the posts.

Solo hitting
This is an excellent, highly recommended batting practice which may also encourage good bowling and fielding. In allowing repeated practice of real skill in a scaled-down version of a major game – playing with classmates of like ability under limited pressure – it is just the type of activity that is needed to realise the performance aims in late Key

Stage 2 and throughout Key Stage 3.

Ideally it is played by five players (*see diagram*), or possibly six in order to be able to divide up a class into viable groups, the sixth acting either as an extra fielder or as an umpire – allowing a simple opportunity for pupils to officiate, as required by the National Curriculum.

The mode of play, rules, etc are exactly the same for both cricket and rounders, the only possible difference being that full-length bowling may be allowed in cricket as an alternative to lobbing the ball from the bowling square or hoop.

A	= Batter
B	= Backstop
C	= Bowler
D, E	= Fielders
○	= Hoops as markers (M)
⟷	= Running

1. The batter **A**, standing to the side of a hoop in **rounders**, and in front of a set of stumps or the equivalent in **cricket**, receives six good balls and attempts to hit each one forward of the line running between the markers **M**.

2. On each successful hit he/she attempts to score as many runs as possible by running to one of the markers **M** (a skittle lying on its side or a hoop), touching it, running back to the centre stumps or hoop, out to the **same** marker, etc, with one run gained for each separate journey.

3. The batter, starting with a credit score of 20, loses, say, three or four runs each time he/she is out, by being caught, run out or, in cricket, bowled.

4. A player may be run out through a direct hit on the hoops, skittles or stumps towards which he/she is running, or the backstop, etc catching the ball and standing in the hoop, touching the skittle, etc.

5. The players rotate in order after a completed 'innings', eg fielder **D** to fielder **E**, fielder **E** to bowler, bowler to batter, batter to backstop, backstop to fielder **D** (or to extra fielder **F** or umpire if six are playing).

Solo mini (or 'diamond') rounders or cricket
The practice is played in groups of four or five, with each player normally receiving from four to six balls in each innings. A softball diamond with shortened distances between the bases is used.

- The batter must always hit the ball forward between the two bases **1** and **3** and then aim to pass as many base markers as possible including that on the 'home' base by running continuously round the diamond until the fielders have completed a set task.

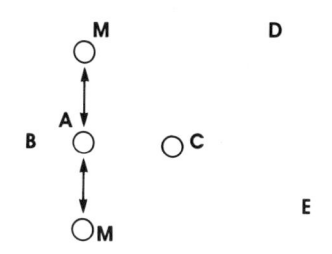

- The task may be as simple as returning the ball to the bowler (or wicket-keeper in cricket), or may involve all the fielding players having to throw and catch in turn once or twice each, or roll the ball from player to player (with all except the player who actually retrieves the ball having to remain stationary).

- The striker loses a number of points for each time he/she is caught out.

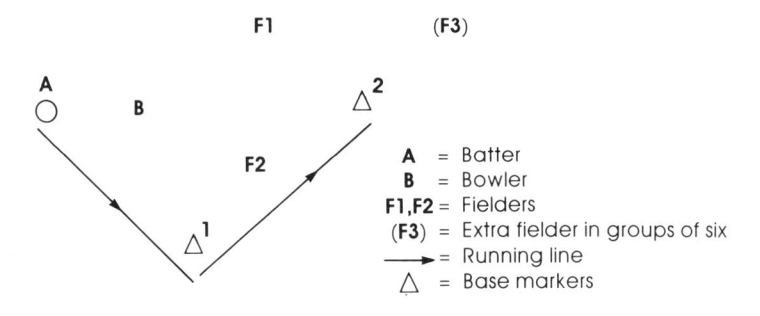

```
                    △³

            F1           (F3)

A                       △²
○     B
              F2         A    = Batter
                         B    = Bowler
                         F1,F2 = Fielders
           △¹            (F3) = Extra fielder in groups of six
                         ──▶  = Running line
                         △    = Base markers
```

Rounders version

- The distance between the bases may be as little as 5 metres but is usually more, say 7–10 metres, to allow for a wider hitting target between bases **1** and **3**.
- If the players are quite young or inexperienced, it may be necessary to use a backstop with fielder **F3** taking over this role.
- The batter stands to the side of a medium or small hoop (*see illustration*), over which the ball should pass and which also acts as the base marker.
- Players may still run on missed balls but with one point deducted.

Cricket version

- The batter defends a set of stumps and, as in other practices, the ball may be lobbed or forced from a higher angle at fairly close range or, more rarely, bowled at full length.
- If the ball is bowled, a wicket-keeper can be used, with **F3** taking over the role.

As the ball can be driven or lofted further, the base distances are normally longer than in the rounders version, with a minimum of 7 metres but more normally 10–12 metres.

These practices maintain a high level of activity and provide varied opportunities for the pupils to experience different skills in simplified but game-relevant situations.

Unit 3 *Rounders-type games*

The vast majority of these games would normally be played with a pitch layout like those described and illustrated in Unit 1.

As suggested, each team member would

- have one turn in each innings
- attempt to negotiate as many posts or markers as possible while the fielding team completes a task
- score one point for each marker passed.

More than one innings may be played. The ball or alternative object to be used should always be hit, thrown, rolled, etc

- forwards over a line which the striker stands behind, or
- more specifically between the first and last markers on the circuit.

The exceptions, such as rounders itself, are indicated.

Passball rounders

Version 1 Beanbag

This game can be used in the earliest phase of Key Stage 2.

1 A beanbag is thrown forwards.
2 The thrower runs round the markers while the fielders retrieve the beanbag and throw it from person to person a given number of times.
3 The number of catches/passes required will depend on the age/skill of the pupils and the distance between the markers, but usually involves five to seven children.
4 The aim is for most pupils to score around the 'middle' range of points, say three or four on a six-marker circuit, and all to be guaranteed at least one point (*see Unit 1*).

Pupils who are fielding are spaced out. They move only

- to retrieve the beanbag when it is thrown out or
- to take a catch or pick up when thrown off-line by a fielder.

Version 2 Ball
1 A small ball may be
   - rolled out along the ground
   - bounced once within a prescribed distance or
   - thrown underhand.

2 Catches or pick-ups are made as in *Version 1*, with number required, distances, etc again matched to ability.

Version 3   Quoit pass rounders
1 A quoit may be rolled or thrown (above or below shoulder height) forwards and catches made by the fielding team as in *Version 1*.

2 The catches may be two-handed or restricted to preferred or non-preferred hand.

3 If pupils are sufficiently skilled, the quoit may be rolled from person to person.

Version 4   Self-hitting
1 The hitter stands on a spot – possibly marked or within a large hoop – holding a fairly soft rubber ball or tennis ball in one hand and a large flat bat in the other.

2 The ball may be bounced or, more usually, thrown up vertically and struck forward.

3 Catching and throwing rules for fielders are as described in *Version 1*.

Version 5   Standard
1 The ball is bowled underarm between knee and shoulder as in full rounders, and to pass over a medium-sized or small hoop (to help regulate the direction).

2 The striker stands at the side of the hoop and hits the ball forwards. The distance between the bowling line or hoop within which the front foot must stay may be the full 7.5 metres as in rounders, or shorter.

3 The game may be played with different equipment according to experience, maturity, etc. For example:
   - initially, a large flat bat and a tennis ball
   - a rounders-type bat (miniature cricket-bat shape) and a tennis ball
   - as ability improves, a rounders ball may be introduced
   - eventually, a rounders stick and ball.

Version 6   Standard plus alternative fielding
Instead of straight throwing and catching by fielders, the ball may be

- bounced from player to player
- rolled from player to player
- rolled or thrown back between the legs by the player in possession.

Version 7   Football passball
1 The ball is kicked forwards by the striker with, normally, no restrictions on height.

2. When kicked the ball is either 'dead' on a prescribed spot, or is rolled gently and evenly towards the kicker (initially the teacher may undertake the rolling for both sides and later, when the speed and direction have been established, the pupils can take over).

3. In fielding, the ball may be brought under control by using any part of the body other than the arms.

4. Passes are made with the feet only, possibly with limitations introduced for higher skill levels, eg only two or one touch(es) allowed.

An interesting alternative is for the striker, after kicking the ball forward, to dribble another ball round the outside of the markers.

Version 8 Hockey pushball

a. The principle is the same as for *Version 7* with a suitable ball, ranging from medium-sized and soft through tennis to a harder hockey ball, hit or pushed out. The fielders use push passes but may graduate to hitting later. Unihoc blades are ideal for Key Stage 2 and early Key Stage 3.

b. As **a**, but with a second ball 'dribbled' round the circuit. The striker either pushes the ball with the stick continuously in contact with the ground, or uses a series of taps.

Version 9 Rugby passball

1. A rugby ball is either thrown or punted out (with marker distances matched accordingly).

2. After a punt out, one punt back towards the mass of fielders may be allowed before restrictions on hands only are imposed.

3. Alternatively all fielders are allowed or forced to punt, thus encouraging a high level of skill in this form of kicking.

There is no reason why any form of game passing cannot be used. For example, it is not difficult to envisage lacrosse, volleyball or basketball techniques being employed in the later stages of Key Stage 3.

Whole team rounders

Teams may have six, eight or ten players, and the game may be played on a circuit as described above or on a normal rounders pitch.

1. One member of the batting team hits the ball forward using any given technique from self-hitting of a tennis ball to a stick with a bowled rounders ball.

Striking and Fielding Games

2 **All** members of the batting team then run round all the posts a number of times (normally two or thee), while the fielding team retrieve the ball and return it to the bowler.

3 The whole fielding team then run and line up (*see diagram*).

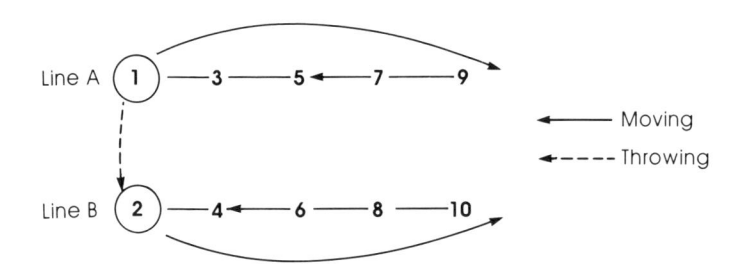

```
Line A  (1)——3——5◄——7——9
                                    ◄———— Moving
                                    ◄---- Throwing
Line B  (2)——4◄——6——8——10
```

4 The ball is thrown from **1** to **2** with **1** immediately running to the back of line A and **3** taking over in the hoop. As soon as **3** is in the hoop, **2** throws and in turn runs to the back of his/her line B, **4** moving forward, and so on. The fielding team score the number of held catches taken with the receiver in a hoop at the point when the last batting team member moves past the last base.

5 The teams then change places and repeat the process, the team with the highest number of catches winning one point.

6 They change places again, another player hits the ball, the fielding/catching and running begins again, and so on until all players have batted.

Alternative versions
- It may be better for the batting team to run individually round the markers, thus saving the slowest from being exposed in finishing last on each run. The hitter runs first, with the second in line starting as soon as a given base is reached, say **2** on the rounders court or **3** on the modified circuit, and so on.

- A football may be used, with the passing being done with the feet. The hoops may be replaced with skittles or posts, with the ball always being passed 'in front' of them.

Skittleball rounders

Standard version
1 An object is placed in the centre of a circle which in turn is in the centre of the rounders circuit. A ball is thrown, hit or kicked (as in *Football passball*) towards the fielders. The type of ball, its size, etc will depend both on ability and on how it is to be propelled.

2 The fielders, using hand passing, aim to hit or knock over the object in the circle before the kicker can run round.

- Both the diameter of the circle and the size of the object can be chosen to suit the skill level of the players and the size of the ball.
- The object is traditionally a skittle (hence the name), ranging in size from a large metal frame type to a small wooden one. Accurate marksmen, however, may be better challenged by something smaller, like a marker dome or even a beanbag.

3 Players are not allowed to run with the ball in hand but fielders not in possession are encouraged to run to good positions to receive a pass and to cover all 'sides' of the circle (*see illustration*).

Alternative version

1 The game can also be played on a whole team basis with as many skittles, posts, etc put in the circle as there are players in each team.

2 The ball is propelled forwards and the fielders aim to knock down as many skittles as possible before the last of the batting team – who all run round – passes the last base.

Football rounders

1 The ball is kicked out as for *Football passball*.

2 The kicker runs round the markers as usual.

3 The fielders aim to bring the ball under control using the body, legs and feet (but not the hands and arms), and with a maximum of three contacts per person, pass the ball as quickly as possible towards the centre of the circuit.

4 It must then be stopped dead inside a circle or a hoop (if inside a circle one fielder may be allowed to move in to trap the ball).

Football or Hockey skittleball rounders

The object is again to hit or knock down a skittle or alternative marker placed inside an appropriately sized circle.

Striking and Fielding Games

- Further limitations, depending on skill levels, understanding, etc can usefully be employed, eg no dribbling, or only two or three contacts allowed then must pass, all passes on the ground or below waist or knee height.
- As with *Skittleball rounders*, fielders are encouraged to 'cover' the circle in case of missed attempts.
- For football: any part of the body other than the arms may be used to bring the ball under control and propel it.

Alternative football version
A whole-team version can be played, with rules as described in the alternative version of *Skittleball rounders*, but played with the feet.

Netball skittleball rounders

As for *Skittleball rounders* but the ball is thrown out and passed using prescribed netball passes only.

Shooting rounders

1 A netball, hockey or soccer ball, etc is hit or propelled forwards and the hitter aims to negotiate as many markers as possible, attempting a second circuit if possible before the fielding team complete their objective.

2 The fielders aim to retrieve the ball, pass to a player in a position to 'score' and then for that player to shoot, aiming to put the ball through a netball ring or into a small goal using a hockey or soccer shot.

The number of players who are allowed to 'score' on any one turn may be restricted to, say, two, with both active in shooting from each side of a goal (which may be improvised from just two high skittles) or alternating when aiming to score in a ring. This allows a balance in terms of ability (say one above and one below average), and enables different pupils to have a go, probably in rotation. Other pupils may be allowed to 'feed' the scorers if the ball runs away.

Dribbling rounders

- As for *Shooting rounders*, except that a designated player has to perform some skills control task such as dribbling through or round a circuit of cones, skittles, etc using hands, feet or a stick.
- The striker may additionally dribble a ball round the bases.
- The dribbling circuit length and difficulty should, as always, be geared to the ability of the pupils and the inter-base distances.

Rounders-type games

Potato race or 'pick-up' rounders

1 A beanbag (or ball) is placed in a hoop at each base.

2 As usual, the striker hits a small ball forwards and the fielders aim to complete a given task involving, say, returning the ball to a circle, passing, etc.

3 The striker may then
   - run to each marker hoop in turn, picking up a beanbag at each and carry them either in the hands or in a suitable container, or
   - as in a potato race and with base distances shortened accordingly, run to base **1**, pick up a bag and return with it to the starting point where it may be either placed or thrown into a bin, then run to base **2**, pick up, return, on to base **3**, etc.

4 The number of points scored is the number of beanbags collected or actually **in** the bin at the point when the fielding team complete the set task.

Alternative objects to collect could be quoits which could be slotted onto a baton carried in one hand, skipping ropes, small balls, small hoops or perhaps even small flags which the children could make and which can be stuck in the ground.

Circle dodgeball rounders

1 Players within a team are paired off with one as striker and the other as the 'dodger'. For teams with odd numbers, one player may act as dodger twice.

2 The dodger takes her/his place in a centrally sited circle (a marked line is best, but a series of marker domes or beanbags can be used) from 3 to 5 metres in diameter. The ball, large or small, is rolled, kicked or hit forward.

3 The hitter attempts to run round the obstacles while the fielders retrieve the ball and return it to players round the circle.

4 The aim is to hit the dodger below the knees or sometimes on the whole leg, using an underarm throw or a controlled push from the chest.

5 The score gained is based on the number of bases passed by the striker when the dodger is hit. It is **vital** that the fielders do not run with the ball.

6 The dodger and the striker then swap roles before the next pair take over.

The competition can be based on the usual team scores or, as an alternative or in addition, on the scores of each pair.

Heading dodgeball rounders

This is an excellent combination of free court dodgeball and rounders.

1 The game is played on a rectangular court with six markers (one at each corner and one halfway down each of the longer sides).

2 The 'heading' team work in pairs with one, the header **H**, standing in a small circle or hoop at the mid-point of one of the shorter sides, the other, the dodger **D**, on the line 2 metres to the left.

3 The ball is lobbed up so that it can easily be headed forward and, as soon as contact is made, **H** starts to run round the circuit and the dodger steps inside the rectangle.

4 The fielders retrieve the ball and aim, without running with it, to pass and hit **D** below the knees, etc.

Fielders may move outside the rectangle but the dodger must remain inside it, being penalised one hit for moving out. Scoring is based on the number of hits recorded before **H** reaches the last post, with the winning team having the lowest total.

Alternative versions
- A light ball may be self-hit with the hand or closed fist, overarm or underarm, etc.
- The ball may be punted out but must be aimed so that it would land in the rectangle.

Running dodgeball rounders

This game can only be played successfully by pupils who are capable of quick movements into space to make a pass and who, in understanding the consequences of a missed attempt to hit the striker, are capable of backing-up in the correct way.

Rounders-type games

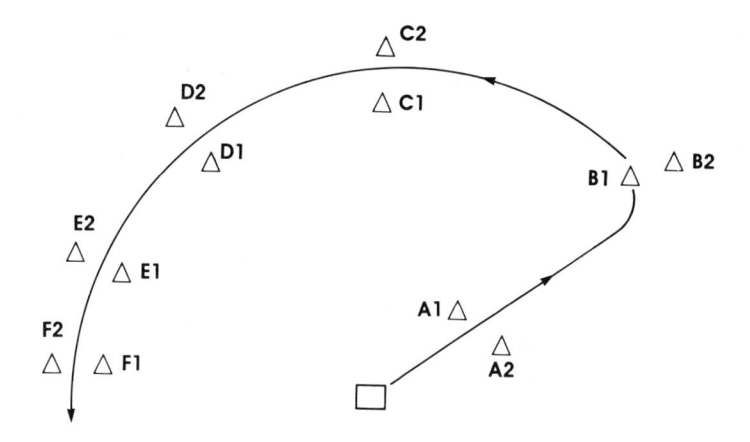

1. The striker, on hitting or kicking the ball forwards, aims to run round the obstacles **A1, B1, C1**, etc.

2. He or she is free to change direction or even stop within the confines of the 'funnel' created by the two sets of markers, but must not move outside it or go back past a marker already passed.

3. Each transgression means a loss of one point from the score.

4. The fielders, using acceptable throws, aim to hit the runner below the knee or on the whole of the leg.

5. The number of points gained are again based on the number of markers passed before the striker is hit.

The fielders, as desired in the National Curriculum, should be helped to become tactically aware. They should learn to either throw 'inwards' from outside the 'funnel' so that a miss can normally be quickly retrieved and through sound passing a second attempt made to hit the runner, or ensure that if thrown from inside the inner markers in an outward direction that another player has moved in line to cover a miss. Failure to do this means that the ball invariably rolls a long way from play and the striker gets maximum points.

Tunnelball rounders

Standard version

This game is an all-time favourite with pupils at Key Stages 2 and 3, and is excellent for keeping fielders active all the time.

1. A large ball is rolled or kicked out forwards and the striker, as usual, attempts to run round the markers.

2. The fielder who first gets hold of the ball keeps it, initially, until all the other fielders run and make a line behind him/her.

Striking and Fielding Games

3 Each pupil stands a metre or less apart with legs apart.

4 The ball is then rolled down the line through all the pairs of legs.

5 The last in the line picks it up and holds it above the head.

- With practice, improved skill and greater maturity, it is possible and obviously time-saving to begin rolling the ball through the first sets of legs in position **before** all the team members are in line. However, it is **essential** that the ball travels through **all** sets of legs and that anyone arriving too late at a centre point in the line must immediately run to the back. If this is not done the striker will be able to run right round and score maximum points. This commonly occurs before the players become adept at the game, and adds to the fun and excitement.

- The first person to field the ball must learn to adopt a sensible position, facing 'outwards', away from as many of the other fielders as possible, and thus shortening the distances that have to be run and the time taken to get into position.

- If the fielders' tunnel crosses the natural running path of the striker, he/she is allowed to run through the line, providing there is a reasonable gap.

- If the line is tightly jammed together and there is no discernible gap, the striker may not push fielders out of the way but must run round the end.

Alternative versions
- A small ball, hit out of the hand or from bowling (tennis or rounders ball, flat or rounders bat), is rolled or passed or (for the more advanced), thrown from hand to hand through the legs. If the ball is dropped, an additional point goes to the striker.

Rounders-type games

- *Archball*
  A large or small ball may be passed or thrown from hand to hand over the head.
- *Relays* may be used to develop skill in tunnelball rounders:

  a The class is divided into teams of four lined up in parallel at least 2 metres apart.
  - The first player in each team has a large ball (or a smaller ball for more advanced pupils) which is held on the ground in front of the feet.
  - On a signal the balls are rolled back through the legs to the end players who pick them up and raise them above the head.
  - Alternatively when the ball reaches the end all the players turn round and the ball is rolled back down the line to the original number **1**.
  - The relay may be repeated with changes in team order.

  b The class is divided into two parallel lines and the balls rolled as above.

  c Two balls are held by the teacher, one in each hand, and on the signal are thrown in different directions. The teams run after the balls, forming lines as quickly as possible and rolling them back through the legs.

Whole team running alternatives

More activity and, sometimes, more interest can be created if the whole of the batting team have to run round the obstacles in a line, particularly if the pupils join hands as in a 'train'. The team run in behind the striker on each turn and the score is the number of markers passed by the last member of the team. If the line breaks, **all** must stop and rejoin – no points for passing markers in broken groups.

Passball, skittleball, circle dodgeball and tunnelball rounders are all suitable games for this alternative.

Multiball rounders

This is an excellent game for enjoyable hitting and fielder activity, with emphasis on developing judgement and accuracy in returning balls.

1 The striker stands next to a container (a small metal or plastic box or bin – if no storage containers are available, a wastepaper bin will do). Depending on age, three or four balls (normally tennis balls but could be rounders balls) are used and are either in the bin or in the striker's non-batting hand.

Striking and Fielding Games

2 The balls, thrown up either directly from the hand or after being picked out of the bin, are hit, normally one at a time (although it is acceptable for two or more to be hit at once), forwards towards the fielders using a flat padder bat or rounders bat as appropriate.

3 On retrieving the balls the fielders aim to return them to two catchers who are stationed close to the container (covered by a 'back-stop' in case of overthrows, etc) and who then put them into the bin.

4 The score obtained by the batter is the number of markers that have been passed when the last ball is returned to the container.

- When hitting, the balls may be 'sprayed' about or all hit in the same direction, thus forcing fielders to run to cover that space.

- Normally if a ball is missed by the hitter, no second attempt is allowed. The ball is dead and is simply picked up by the catchers.

- There is a premium on the fielders not simply to return a ball accurately to the catchers but to ensure that they are in a position to receive it. Four balls all returned at once at the same pace through the air produce chaos, and it is necessary for pupils to learn, through calling or signals, who is to throw to whom and when, and to vary the form of the return. For example, a slow roll used at the same time as a sharp throw would help to alleviate the problem.

This is an excellent example of the sort of game, suited to National Curriculum demands, that stresses intelligent hitting and accurate, properly timed, fielding returns.

Rounders-type games

Scatterball

This game is based on the principle of *Multiball rounders*, but allows all the players on both sides to be active throughout.

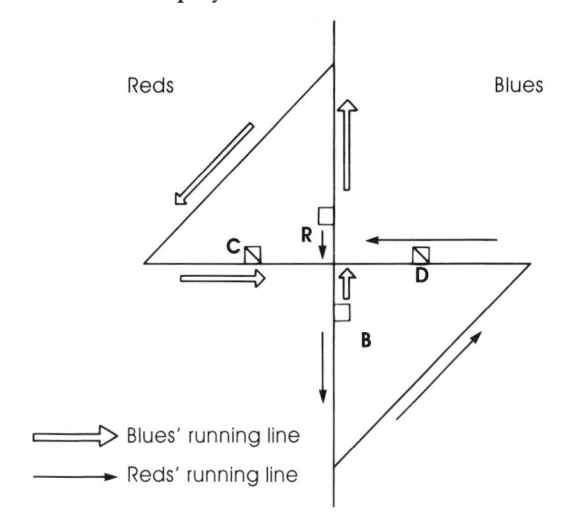

⇒ Blues' running line
→ Reds' running line

1. The field or court is divided into two halves, each half being exclusive fielding territory for one of the teams, the blues or the reds. It is possible to have circuits of different shapes, eg a square.

2. All the red players except the batter **R** are spread out in the red half of the court and, similarly, the blues apart from batter **B** are spaced out in their own section.

3. Each batter has an equal number of balls and on a given signal hits all of them one at a time into the opposition half and, carrying the bat, aims to run round the triangle marked out in the opponents' section to pass a container, **C** or **D** as appropriate, before the opposing team can collect all the balls and put them in it.

Scoring can be done in a variety of ways:

- A point may be awarded to the team which either fills the bin or has a batter home first.

- Each batter can score a point if he/she can pass the bin before all the balls are returned.

- In addition, a point can be given to the first team to get all balls into the bin.

- As in *Multiball rounders* a number of markers, say five or six, are used, with both batters scoring the number passed before the bin is filled (with or without a bonus for the first bin filled).

Striking and Fielding Games

Pinball rounders

This really excellent game involves all players all of the time, and combines rounders with 'invasion' game passing. Each game involves three teams of, ideally, four or five players, so for normal classes two or more games can be run in parallel.

1. A six-marker circuit as described in Unit 1 is used, with a marked circle in the centre. Inter-base distances and circle diameter will depend on both skill levels and chosen objective.

2. Assume that team **R**, the reds, bat first with team **B**, the blues, and **G**, the greens, both fielding.

3. The ball, large or small, is propelled forwards in some way either out of the hand or, more usually, from a bowl or roll (a bowler is selected from the blues) using a kick or a hit.

4. The batter tries to run round all the markers while the fielders collect the ball and using below-head passing aim to bring the ball to the circle where it may be passed to a blues team member or used to hit a skittle, etc.

5. The major difference in this game is that the remaining three or four red team members are out on the court trying to intercept the ball or to legally prevent a player from passing, in order help the team mate who is running round.

6. If the ball is successfully intercepted, the striker may continue to run round and score maximum points, or the interceptor may be required to pass it immediately to another opposition (blues or greens) team member.

7. When all reds have batted, blues take over as striker plus interceptors, with greens providing bowler (and backstop if required), etc.

It is essential that the batting team at least can be identified – through wearing bibs, etc.

Danish rounders

This is a game for well-prepared classes in Key Stage 3, or team squads with many pupils capable of fast, accurate throwing and good catching.

1. A square or diamond-shaped pitch (both involving four bases) could be used, or a modified rounders court including the hitting box (five bases) or a rectangle (six bases – *see below*).

2. Distances between bases can be varied but the basic rounders 'gap' of around 12 metres is a good starting point.

3 Each base is placed in a medium-sized hoop and a fielder stationed at each.

4 Ideally the game is played with two teams of 8–11, depending on the number of bases being used. In order to allow everyone to experience all roles, including, possibly, umpire, it can also be played in solo form.

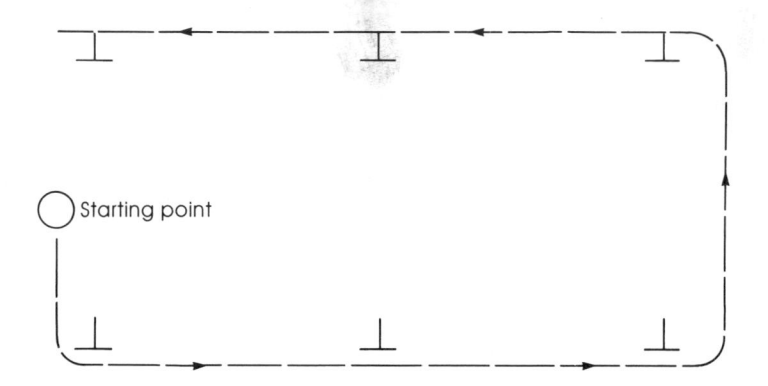

5 The ball (tennis or rounders) is bowled in the usual way to a batter standing in a square or beside a hoop midway between two of the bases or, in the case of a rounders court, in the normal batting square.

6 The batter attempts to run round all the bases and, depending on the fielders' ability, possibly return to the starting square or hoop.

7 Any fielder may retrieve the ball and must throw it quickly to the nearest base.

8 The ball is then thrown round all the bases, aiming to 'beat' the runner. In each case a base's foot must be in the hoop.

There is clearly some emphasis on both speed and accuracy in that time spent 'chasing' a ball, and returning it to a base is time wasted – the faster the throw, the turn, etc, the better the chance of beating the runner.

On a rounders pitch, another player moves up as a base fielder into the batting square (with hoop) after the ball is hit.

Alternative version
At a simpler level the ball may be thrown, bounced or rolled out.

Some of the games described above may be adapted for indoor use by using a 'gamester' or airflow ball.

Striking and Fielding Games

Rounders – the standard game

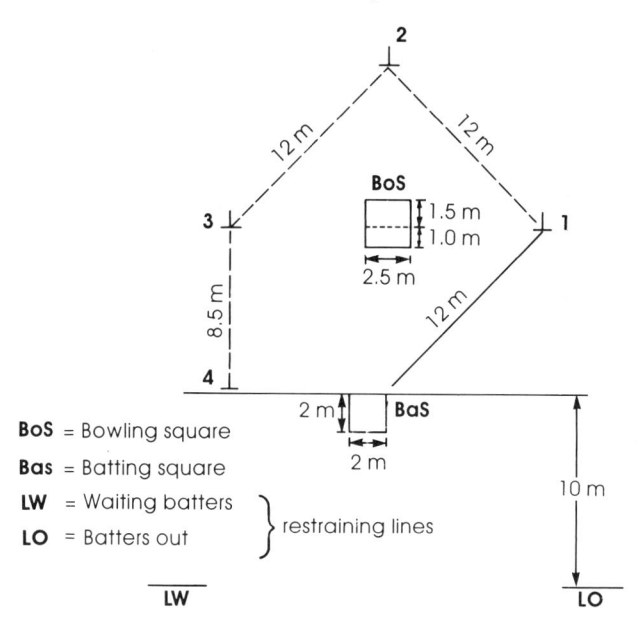

BoS = Bowling square
Bas = Batting square
LW = Waiting batters
LO = Batters out
} restraining lines

The continuous lines signify compulsory markings.
1, 2, 3 and 4 are the posts.

Teams: Maximum nine players with two substitutes for bona fide matches. More, with all playing, could take part in lessons to suit group numbers.

Innings: Each team is allowed up to two innings in a standard match with the innings closing when the last player is out.

Rules

Complete rules are available from the National Rounders Association – *see Appendix 1*.

Batting

1. The batter must stand with both feet **in** the batting square and must not cross the front or back lines when hitting the ball.

2. The batter receives one **good** ball only and must run for first base regardless of whether or not contact is made.

3. The batter may take a no-ball and score in the usual way. The no-ball is deemed to have been taken if the hitter comes within reach of the first base.

4. If only one batter is left in, he/she has a choice of three good balls. Remaining balls are forfeited if a hit is caught or a ball is taken (if as with a no-ball, the batter runs to within reach of the first base). A one-minute rest is allowed if a rounder is scored.

5 A batter is **out** if
- the ball is caught from a hit made by bat/stick or hand, except from a no-ball
- the foot moves over the front or back batting square lines before hitting the ball, except on a no-ball
- he/she runs to the inside of a post or past the post on the inside, except when obstructed
- if a fielder touches a post with the ball or hand holding the ball before the runner approaching that post touches it, except in the case of first post after a no-ball
- he/she loses contact with the post (or runs) when the bowler has the ball and is in the bowling square or during the bowler's action before the ball is actually released
- the bat is dropped or thrown deliberately
- he/she overtakes a player who is running in front.

A **side** is out if, when there are no players waiting to bat, the ball is either thrown full pitch or is placed by a fielder in the batting square before any batter reaches fourth base.

No-ball

A no-ball is a ball that is

- not delivered with a smooth continuous underarm action
- bowled with any part of a foot **over** the bowling square line
- higher than the batter's head or lower than the knee when it passes the batter, is wide, or is on the non-hitting side of the batter, or hits (or would hit) the batter if avoiding action wasn't taken.

Procedure/Running

- A batter at a base may run on a no-ball, regardless of whether the ball is taken by the batter taking strike, and he/she is then subject to normal rules.
- A batter may choose not to run unless the batter on the base behind him is obliged to run. Only one batter is allowed on one base at a time.
- A batter stopping at any base **must** touch the post with bat or hand and maintain contact with it until another run is made.
- The fourth base post **must** always be touched with bat or hand for a rounder to be scored.
- If a player has left the previous post when the bowler gets possession of the ball whilst in the square, he/she must continue to the next post and can be put out in the normal way.

- If a ball is hit behind the line running through the front edge of the batting square (ie into the backward area), the batter may only proceed to the first base, until the ball is returned into the forward area when normal rules again apply (eg a missed ball by the bowler or other fielders may give the batter the opportunity to move to the second base).

- While waiting to bat or having been given out, all batters must remain behind the marked line 10 metres into the backward area. If a player comes forward of this line and obstructs the fielders then either half a rounder is given to the fielding team or, if the batting team had gained a rounder, it is declared void and the obstructor is given out.

Scoring

- One rounder is scored if a batter having hit the ball succeeds in running round the track and touching fourth post (or from first post after a backward hit), either running non-stop or, if there is a stop at any base en route, if the post immediately ahead has not been touched by a fielder with the ball.

- A half rounder is scored if a batter missing the ball runs and fulfills the above conditions.

- A penalty half rounder is awarded
  – when the bowler delivers consecutive no-balls to the same batter
  – for obstruction as described above.

Variations

Stopping rounders

The game is based on normal rounders with the following variations:

- Batters do not have to run on when another player runs to the base they are currently occupying. Thus there can be many batters standing waiting at the same base.

- Batters are also out if, when the bowler receives the ball in the bowling square and calls out 'Stop!', they are still running between bases.

Three-ball rounders

This game may be played on a normal rounders pitch or on a square as for *Danish rounders*, using posts, hoops, etc with a full nine a side or down to as low as six.

- Each batter is entitled to three good balls, and endeavours to score a rounder by reaching base **4** either directly from one hit or after stopping at any of the preceding bases.

- If a player is out (in any of the usual ways, or restricted to catching and base stumping only) on balls 1 or 2, he/she goes to the back of the batting line but still receives the remaining ball(s).
- In the smaller team versions, base fielders are expected to chase some balls, being temporarily replaced by a centrally situated fielder or even the bowler.

Sector rounders

This is the same as for the full game or the variations above, with extra points being scored if the ball is hit into one or a number of marked areas (using marker domes, beanbags, etc) as designated by the teacher.

Rounders and its variations can also be played using different bats and balls, particularly bigger bats and larger and/or softer balls for young children.

Unit 4 *Cricket-type games*

The object of this unit is to show how skills can be used in games which, by ensuring a high degree of activity for all players involved, are very suitable for use in games lessons and in some forms of representative matches. The majority are solo or pairs, rota-based, scaled-down versions of the full game, which allow experience in many roles and are particularly well suited to the latter part of Key Stage 2 and the whole of Key Stage 3. Some games which have a looser connection with cricket and which can be played for fun are also included.

Equipment used will depend on

a the level at which the game is being played – that is, the point within a given Key Stage, and

b the safety factor (that is, taking into account the distance between games when more than one is being played).

The following combinations may be used.

- a cricket bat and cricket ball (or an alternative hard ball)
- a cricket bat and solid rubber ball
- a cricket bat or wooden bat shape and tennis ball
- a plastic bat and ball (*see Kwik cricket* below).

The size of the bat to be used should be geared to the age/size of the person batting and size of ball, and the length of the pitch geared to the age group or span taking part (*see Appendix 2*). If a hard ball is being bowled then protective clothing should be worn by batters and wicket-keepers (*see Unit 7*).

Rota cricket

Pairs

1 The game is played in groups of eight divided into four matched pairs.

2 One pair, in this case **B1** and **B2**, are batting at any given time.

3 Another pair comprises the wicket-keeper (**W**) and the fielder square of the wicket (**Fw**), who may change over halfway through each set of overs.

4 A third pair consists of a bowler (**Bo**) and a fielder (**Fbo**) behind the wicket at the opposite end, who bowl alternate overs in the set.

5 The fourth pair are two out and out fielders who operate in front of the wickets (**F1** and **F2**).

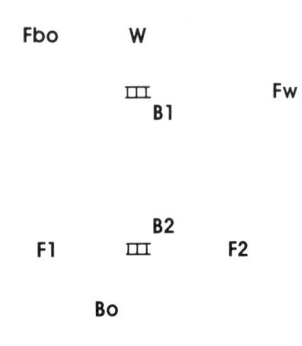

Cricket-type games

6 The four fielding positions are set for a right-handed batter. They are 'reversed' for a left-handed player, and may be changed to cater for given players' strengths.

7 One or more can eventually be placed by the bowler when a basic tactical understanding has been acquired.

After the batters receive their allocated number of overs, all pairs rotate and take on a new role and so on until all players have had an opportunity to bat, bowl and field and at least four – possibly all eight – to act as wicket-keeper.

8 The batters can play as normal, receiving a total of four, six or eight overs between them, depending on the time available. However, as it is quite probable that one batter will receive many more balls than the other, it is possible to divide the bowling equally between the two, with each facing alternate overs. A batter who scores an odd number of runs must go back to the 'receiving' end for the next ball.

9 Each pair continues to receive all the allotted balls even if they are 'out', but lose a number of runs each time this happens. The number depends very much on the ability of the players and the number of runs being scored in total, but will probably be between three and six.

10 In order to avoid the possibility of a negative score through being out early in the innings, all batters start with a runs 'credit' (as in the batting practice described in Unit 2), the amount being related to the number of runs lost when out, say from 20 up to 100.

The competition is obviously between the pairs, the winners being the two batters with the highest combined score. It is also possible to have a bowling champion pair for the most wickets taken, or a bowling/fielding championship for the smallest total number of runs against.

Solo

This is the original game upon which *Pairs* is based. The game is virtually the same, except that there is only one batter playing at one time, who can only be run out at the end he/she is running to.

- Each batter has two or four overs, split evenly between two bowlers who work in tandem at opposite ends.

- The next player to bat pads up ready to go in as soon as the innings is finished and then fields behind the wicket on the leg side from where the first over is faced.

The competition is thus an individual one, with everyone rotating after each completed innings.

Alternative bowling arrangement

In both the *Pairs* and *Solo* games it is possible to speed up the 'action' by having two bowlers at the same end at the same time.

1 They bowl alternately with one being ready to start the run-up as soon as the previous ball is on its way directly to the other (eg rolled back from a four or thrown by a close fielder after a defensive shot).

2 If the batter is to receive two overs, all bowling can take place from one end – saving time on changing over. If batters receive four overs, two overs will be from each end, with either two different bowlers operating (with each bowling to two different batters), or the original pair moving to the other end and bowling another over each. In this case, after completion of the overs, **one** bowler goes back to the original end to start another block of two, the other being replaced on an overlap system.

Regardless of the system, eventually all players bowl the same number of overs as each batter receives.

Six-a-side (pairs) cricket

The rules are virtually the same as for *Pairs rota cricket*, except that there are two complete sides of six.

1 Each is divided into three pairs, with one pair from the batting team completing the allotted number of overs and being replaced by the second pair from that team, etc.

2 On the fielding team the two players who have just completed the allotted bowling span move on to replace the two fielders who in turn replace the wicket-keeper/fielder, who in turn become the new bowlers.

3 The combined scores of each set of three batting pairs gives the separate team totals.

4 The four players on the batting team who are not batting at any given time can be given 'active' roles with one pair possibly acting as umpires and the other as scorers.

This is an excellent example of the small-side game advocated in the National Curriculum Programmes of Study. It guarantees practice in applied skills, allowing opportunities for changing bowling and field placings in the light of evaluating batting techniques ('decision making'). Pupils also learn more about the game through applying rules and making decisions as umpires and possibly communicating information to scorers.

Eight-a-side cricket

Each team is divided into four pairs with each pair batting for four or five overs in a 16- or 20-over game.

1. Each team starts its innings with a credit score of 200 runs. The batters have unlimited lives but for each dismissal eight runs are deducted from the team total.

2. When a batter loses a life he/she may not face the next ball and the players change ends, except after a 'dismissal' on the last ball of an over.

3. Each player on the fielding team must bowl a minimum of one over and no one player can bowl more than three overs in a 16-over match or four overs in a 20-over match.

4. No fielder except the wicket-keeper is allowed to field nearer than 10 metres in front of the bat or anywhere on the leg side, as measured from the stumps (*see Unit 7*).

Apart from these, normal rules and procedure apply.

Softball cricket

This game, using a worn tennis ball and 'junior' stumps, and played on a 15-metre pitch, is particularly suited to Key Stage 2 development.

1. Each team of eight players has one innings of 12 or 16 overs. The batting team are again divided into pairs with each pair batting for three overs (in the 12-over game) or four overs (16-over game).

2. No player may bowl more than three overs (12-over game) or four overs (16-over game), and the wicket-keeper does not bowl.

3. Each team starts with a score of 200, with six runs being deducted for each wicket that falls.

4. Again, after a dismissal, the batter who was 'out' may not face the next delivery and thus changes ends, except on the last ball of an over.

Kwik cricket

This game, which is highly successful in both Australia and New Zealand, has been specially designed for primary age pupils and therefore has enormous value for work in Key Stage 2.

- The equipment is made of toughened plastic with a basic set consisting of just two bats, two sets of stumps and two balls (*see Appendix 1*).

Striking and Fielding Games

- The bats are light and therefore easy to handle, the stumps have a hollow base which can be filled or part-filled with sand or water to increase stability, and the balls, while simulating the bounce of a 'proper' ball, are soft and cannot be hit too far, thus removing the need for protective clothing, and allowing games and practices to be played in quite small areas.
- The game can be played on any flat surface.

The rules for the various games are similar to those described above.

1. Each player bats for a minimum of two overs; each player bowls a minimum of one over; each player or batting pair starts with 200 runs and loses six runs for each time out; players change ends each time a batter is out, except on the last ball of the over.

2. A major difference is that players **cannot** be out Leg Before Wicket (LBW).

Several games can be played:

Kwik singles, in groups of around six with all players rotating and each batter receiving a minimum of one over from two different bowlers.

Kwik pairs, in groups of 8–12 with each pair, as above, batting, fielding and bowling, but also taking an over each as wicket-keeper and, possibly, in the larger units taking a turn as umpire.

Kwik team, with two teams of 6–8 players, each pair batting in turn and adding up the scores for a team total and all players fielding.

Kwik cricket, played with teams of 8–12 players, each pair batting in turn but not fielding with the opponents.

In the last two games the next batting pair always act as umpires.

When a school only has one set of equipment and wishes the pupils to gain experience by playing in smaller units, eg *Kwik pairs* in a group of eight, the activity may be incorporated into groupwork with, for example, two sets of four pupils combining to compete in the pairs activity (*see Unit 7*).

Eleven-a-side cricket

Although the games described above allow for guaranteed participation for each player, and more activity generally, and are strongly recommended for players in Key Stages 2 and 3, some pupils may not perceive them as the 'real' game and may occasionally enjoy taking part in a full-sided match, providing that it is outside lesson time.

- While playing normal rules and using normal scoring with normal dismissals, it is still possible to introduce conditions which will ensure that more players are guaranteed an active part in the game. The simplest method is to use National Knockout Cup restrictions and limit bowlers to a given number of overs, ensuring that at least five are used. This can be extended up to the point (see *Eight-a-side cricket*) where all players except the wicket-keeper bowl – say two overs each in a 20-over game.

- Batting time can also be loosely restricted by adopting a system used in some local competitions where a batter must 'retire' when he/she reaches a given score, say 20 or 25 runs, but is allowed back in if one of the last official pair is out before the allotted number of overs have been bowled.

Resolving a tie

A tie may stand in a class or league match, but in a knockout game where it is not possible to replay, some acceptable and quick method of producing a winner is needed.

- If time allows, a short four- or six-over game can be played with four or six players bowling one over each and two or three pairs each batting for two overs.

- A quick method involving cricket skills is for all the six or eight team members to bowl, throw or even roll the ball at one set of stumps from behind the opposite end batting crease. In the event of equal scores being obtained, the bowling/throwing/rolling continues on a sudden-death basis (as used in a soccer penalty knockout) until one player hits and the other side's representative fails.

- A very simple method for younger players is to have a speed rolling competition with three or four players at each end of the pitch, each rolling the ball in turn (see *diagram*). The ball must cross the batting crease before it can be picked up and is rolled back from the other side of the stumps. This method may also be used in the event of equal scores after bowling or throwing at the stumps, particularly if the scores are low.

H G F E   A B C D

----▶ Rolling ball

Striking and Fielding Games

Non-stop cricket

This is an excellent fun game both for outside and indoors (sports hall, gym and if using a sponge or an airflow ball, the school hall).

- Teams may be of any number above six (8–11 is best).
- A tennis ball is used with a proper bat or shape.
- The layout is as shown below, and rules must be strictly adhered to.

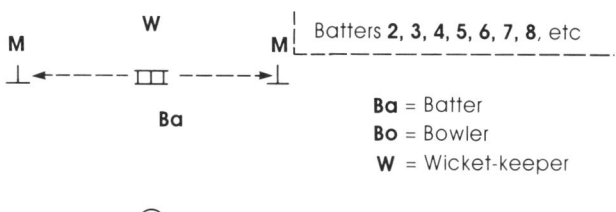

```
              W                   |  Batters 2, 3, 4, 5, 6, 7, 8, etc
    M                          M  |
    ⊥ ←---- ▥ ----→ ⊥
                                   Ba = Batter
              Ba                   Bo = Bowler
                                   W  = Wicket-keeper

              ○
              Bo
```

1 Each batter, on hitting the ball or if the ball hits any part of the legs, must run round or touch one of the markers **M** (hoops, bat shapes or skittles laid on the ground, or posts) and aim to return to the wicket as quickly as possible.

2 The bowler must keep at least one foot in a marked bowling circle, square or hoop. He or she can bowl the ball at the stumps regardless of whether the batter has returned. The ball must be bowled underhand and must bounce before hitting the stumps, or the batter is not out.

3 If the ball is not hit and misses the stumps, the batter does not run.

4 The batter, on just making it back to make a hit while still running, may continue moving in the same direction to the opposite marker.

5 When a batter is out by being bowled, by hitting the wicket or by being caught (there is no stumping or run-out possible), the next batter must get the bat from the player who is just out and prepare to face the bowling immediately. As already stated, the bowler can bowl as soon as the ball is in his/her hands, whether or not the crease is occupied. It is thus possible to be out before you are 'in'. The process continues with sometimes more than one player being out before the ball is hit.

6 Each bowler is limited to a six-ball over and must be replaced by another player when this is completed. The whole fielding team should know the order in which they bowl, with the next replacement always being ready to take over, so that no opportunity of bowling a batter out is wasted.

7 The penalty for bowling more than the allotted six balls, or bowling again before everyone else in the team has had an over, is quite severe. Each additional ball is in effect a no-ball – runs can be scored, but if the ball or bat hits the stumps or a catch is given, the batter is not out.

The teacher or children sitting out may count the balls and, when first playing the game, announce the completion of each over up to, say, four, until the routine is established.

8 The batter can score runs off a full toss but may not be out bowled or to a catch (the ball **must** bounce).

9 Catches may be made from balls rebounding from walls and ceilings.

The distance from the stumps (springback, blocked or skittles indoors) to the markers will vary according to the setting, pupil ability and whether a touch or running round is required. It may range from 3–4 metres inside, where the hitting distance is limited and rebounds may aid the bowling side, to possibly double this outside. The bowling distance can vary from 5 to 8 metres.

For indoor play many floors will need protecting from damage by the bat. Some type of smooth, tough plastic, rubber or fibre mat may be used of sufficient length to allow the ball to always pitch on it and not to shoot up off its leading edge.

Non-stop football cricket

As for *Non-stop cricket*, with the ball being either

- rolled along the ground or gently bounced in delivery, or
- fielded and returned using any part of the body.

Players giving catches or touching the stumps with the feet are out, as normal.

Football cricket

A pitch can be set up on any reasonably flat piece of ground, or the game can be played indoors in a sports hall or large gym.

1 There are two sets of stumps from 9 to 15 metres apart and normally two teams of from 8 to 11 players, although the game can be played on a rota basis.

2 The 'bowlers' standing behind a line or in a hoop 6–8 metres from each set of stumps roll or more usually bounce a large plastic ball or football in six-ball overs alternately towards each wicket. The 'batters' defend the stumps and

on kicking the ball must run, crossing over in the usual way.

3 A batter can be out
- if the ball when bowled hits the stumps
- by being run out:
  simple version – when the ball hits the stumps after any kind of return involving any part of the body
  advanced version – with no contact with the hands and arms and returning the ball through kicking (one or two players normally remain within close distance of the stumps in order to 'push' the ball onto them after it has been kicked in)
- caught out (simple version)
- if one contact is made with the forehead or with a foot to a ball off the ground (advanced version) or, more demanding, the ball can be kept off the floor and control demonstrated by a player – this may vary with ability but, for example, could be as simple as one clean header into the air or could involve flicking up with the foot or kneeing the ball to be followed by a header to demonstrate that the ball is under control.

4 The whole team is out if three players can either each make contact with the ball before it touches the ground or a wall, etc or, at a higher skill level, the second and third contacts demonstrate control.
- In the advanced version a penalty of six runs is given to the batting team each time a fielder deliberately handles the ball.
- Batters usually retire on reaching a score of 15 or 20.
- More than one innings may be played.

Heading cricket

Basically the format is as for *Football cricket*, with the following changes.

- The 'bowling' becomes a 'service', with the ball lobbed up so that it is dropping onto the batter's head at crease distance (about 1 metre) from the stumps.

- Balls reaching the batter at lower than head height are no-balls, with headers allowed to choose to run if they wish after heading them. They cannot be out as a direct result of heading this type of ball but may, as in all forms of cricket, be run out after opting to run.

- The distance between the stumps may be shortened.

- A greater stress may be put on heading in the field, demonstrating contact, or full control, as the means of getting a player or team out.

Unit 5 Longball, softball, stoolball and minor games

Longball

Longball, sometimes known as *Swedish longball*, is an exciting and excellent hitting game, demanding at its highest level very quick-moving and accurate throwing from the fielders, and intelligent and decisive running from the hitters. It can be enjoyed in some form by pupils working at the top end of Key Stage 2 through to Key Stage 4 (year 6 onwards), and can be modified to suit different spaces available, different numbers of players and for playing indoors in a sports hall or large gym.

The basic court is a rectangle of 40 by 20 metres, each corner being marked with a rounders base or skittle. The 40-metre lines are called side lines but these are not essential and the game can be played without using them. One 20-metre line is called the base line and the other the end line.

Ideal team numbers are 10–12 but a class of 30+ can be divided into two halves and the game still enjoyed. Alternatively the class can be divided into three teams with two playing each other at *Longball* and one team playing a solo version of, say, a rounders-type game.

1 The fielding or 'out' team has one backstop standing approximately 5 metres behind the base line at the halfway point (ie 10 metres in) and opposite the bowler who is 8 metres in the field of play standing with the front foot, at least, in a marked square or a hoop.

2 The other team members are spaced evenly about the playing area with one, ideally, standing just within each of the markers on the base line.

3 The batting or 'in' team have one player ready to strike, standing slightly to the side of a small marked square or hoop at the midpoint of the base line.

Ba = Backstop   **B** = Batter   **Bo** = Bowler
R = Batting team restraining area

Striking and Fielding Games

4. The remainder of the team stand just behind the line, at least 3 metres to the striker's left. (In the simple version these players can sit down or stand some metres behind the line.)

5. Each hitter normally carries the bat (flat padder, rounders or stoolball) when running.

6. It is essential in the full game, and helpful in the simple version, that the two teams, wearing bibs or braids, can be easily identified.

7. The ball, normally a tennis ball or, alternatively, a fairly soft rubber ball – but **not** a rounders ball or any other hard ball – is bowled between knee and shoulder and must pass over the marked square or hoop to be 'good'.

8. The hitter receives one 'good' ball and runs regardless of whether or not the ball is struck.

9. A 'bad' ball becomes 'good' if it is struck.

Simple version

1. The batter attempts to hit the ball forward of the base line and to run down the field of play to cross the end line into safe territory.

2. He/she is out if
   - the ball is caught
   - the ball is hit behind the base line
   - he/she is hit by the ball before gaining the safety of the end line – the vital component of the game.

3. The batter decides whether to stay in the end zone – the more usual course – or to run back **immediately** and attempt to cross the base line without being hit. No interval is allowed.

4. If staying, the player waits until the next striker or any subsequent player attempts a hit, remaining there as long as he/she likes.

5. The batter **must** cross the end and base lines **between** the two markers. Passing on the wrong side of the marker means that the runner **must** retrace his/her steps, come back on to the pitch, and cross the line at some point between the markers before being hit.

6. One point is scored by returning to the base line after a break in the end zone, and two points if returning immediately. No points are scored for simply reaching the end line.

7. When three or four players are out, the teams change over. The game is thus continuous, with all players always

batting in order and the next player due to strike when a team is out being the first batter when that team gains another innings.

8 The score is cumulative.

- If the batter misses the ball, the backstop has an excellent opportunity to score a direct hit on the player's back, etc from behind as he/she runs down the court, or to throw the ball quickly to the bowler or other fielders en route for them to attempt a hit from closer range.

- An alternative rule which encourages risk-taking is that anyone waiting behind the end line is also out (as being 'in' the game) when a batter is out to a catch, etc with, possibly, teams changing when a higher total number are out, say five.

Full version

Invariably chaotic when classes first attempt it, the game is worth persevering with as, eventually, the players grasp what is required and will find it highly enjoyable.

1 Players may still be out as individuals to a catch, or for hitting behind.

2 The **essential** difference is that in this, the real game, if a player is hit with the ball while in the field of play, the whole of the 'out' team must run and endeavour to get behind the base line – running between the markers – before any member of the 'in' team can retrieve the ball and hit one of them with it.

3 If all the 'out' players succeed in making it home without being hit, they become the 'in' team and proceed to bat.

4 If, however, one is hit before crossing the base line, his/her team (currently the 'outs') attempt to get the ball and hit one of the current 'ins' who have moved on to the court – before they all get back.

5 The first team to get back **untouched** become the batters.

Changes can occur rapidly with up to three reversals following one hit being common, leading to high excitement and, naturally, mistakes. It must be stressed that once a team member has thrown the ball and hit a member of the opposition in the field of play, no member of the thrower's team must then voluntarily touch the ball. By doing so, through being the last to have any contact with the ball, the team they are in automatically become the 'outs'. It is very common in the early stages for fielders to pick up the ball after the batter has been hit but, eventually, they learn to resist the temptation. Often the same team gains consecutive innings.

Striking and Fielding Games

- It may appear at first sight that this game, apart from the controlled batting required, lacks skill, with a lot of wild running and luck (combined with some accuracy) in hitting a runner. Nothing could be further from the truth. Well-prepared groups soon learn that it is very much a moving game, with players rapidly taking up new positions and moving the ball about, often with fast, short passes, in order to cut runners off (no player is allowed to run with the ball). Specifically, they learn to 'cover' the lines, particularly the base line, to stop players scoring, and eventually to 'attack' the runner by pursuing him/her back into space.

- When players are forced back from the lines in order to avoid being hit and, particularly, when, as is simpler, no side lines are used, a type of stalemate can result. This is easily resolved by giving the runner a time limit (normally 5–10 seconds and often counted out loud) within which an attempt must be made to cross the line. Players will almost always make the attempt, but if not the player holding the ball when the time expires simply drops (not throws) it.

- It should be noted that when a running batter is hit in the field area close to the end line, it is essential that that player, as the only 'in' player near the ball, immediately attempts to retrieve it and return it hard and fast to team mates crossing the base line.

- Players may not necessarily be out to a catch – although they usually are (plus possibly any waiting in the end zone). A catch may simply be accepted as giving the 'out' team a better opportunity of hitting the runner.

Stoolball

Stoolball is an excellent marriage between cricket and rounders which is suited to players working on Key Stages 3 and 4 and, in modified form, for Key Stage 2 (see *Mini-stoolball*).

In the authorised 'correct' form of the game, special stoolball equipment must be used, specific rules adhered to, and as in cricket, side numbers are restricted to a maximum of eleven. However, as with the vast majority of summer games, it is possible to improvise.

1 Ideally a proper stoolball bat with a wide, round, thick blade, and a ball which is similar in appearance and density to a rounders ball, but larger, should be used and, if the game is to be played regularly, it is worth investing in this equipment and buying or making the special wickets described below.

2 In improvised forms of the game, a rounders or flat padder bat may be used with a tennis or rounders or baseball ball.

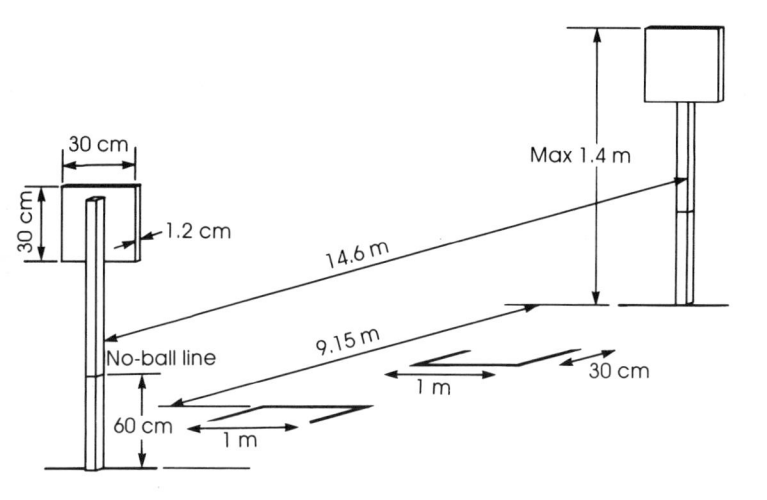

3 As shown (*see diagram*), the game requires two 'wickets' in the form of square boards mounted on stable posts, which may be set in the ground or are portable. Stoolball posts may be bought or improvised by attaching a piece of 30 cm² hardboard to a suitable post or stand. The top edge should be no more than 1.4 metres from the ground.

4 The wickets are placed a maximum of 14.6 metres apart in the centre of a large playing area, normally a field but possibly a big playground or all-weather area.

5 There are two bowling creases, one metre in length, each placed 9.15 metres from a wicket.

6 The boundary line, if used (see scoring below), is 40 metres.

The following rules are essential to the game.

1 The ball must be bowled underhand with both feet behind the bowling crease and must be deemed to be in reach of the batter.
   - If thrown below a height of 60 cm (50 cm in *Mini-stoolball*) the ball is a **no-ball**; if it is thrown too high or out of normal reach of the sides, it is a **wide ball**.
   - Both no-balls and wide balls count as one run but, if wides are hit, they count as normal balls and are subject to normal rules.

59

2. Runs are scored by hitting the ball anywhere in the field of play, the two batters crossing and touching the **face** of the wicket with the bat (not the post).
   - All runs may be obtained through running, with no limit to the number that can be scored from one hit, or a boundary may be used with scoring as in cricket (ie with fours and sixes).
   - Byes may also be scored from 'good' balls missed by the fielders.

3. An innings may be played out until one player remains as in cricket or, to ensure that more players get an opportunity, batters may compulsorily retire on a given score, say 15, 20 or 25.

4. Batters are out
   - if the ball when bowled hits any part of the face of the wicket – but not the post
   - if the ball when struck is caught
   - if in running, starting out to run, or moving at any time beyond the point where the wicket face can be touched with the bat, the ball is thrown or, if held in the hand, touched onto the face of the wicket (but not the edge or back) before the batter can touch it with the bat
   - if the batter stops the ball hitting the wicket with any part of the body or the bat when running.

5. Batters are not out
   - if caught or bowled on a no-ball
   - if obstructed by a fielder in any way and at any point.

6. Eight-ball overs are bowled alternately to each end. No player may bowl consecutive overs.

Clearly many of the fielding and batting practices described in Unit 2 would be of great value for *Stoolball*. As, however, all skill is highly specific, it would be necessary to use a stoolball ball and bat in the later phases of the practices and these in turn would need to be adapted to take into account the particular nature/height, etc of the special wickets used in the game.

Mini-stoolball

For younger players – certainly in Key Stage 2 and possibly moving into Key Stage 3 (say up to year 8) – *Mini-stoolball* should be played. This game is the same as *Stoolball* but with a number of reductions in scale. Wickets are 1.2 metres high, the distance between the wickets is 10 metres, the bowling creases are 6 metres from the wickets, and the boundary, if used, is a maximum of 30 metres.

Longball, softball, stoolball and minor games

Non-stop stoolball
The rules are the same as for *Non-stop cricket* (see *Unit 4*), only using stoolball wickets and, preferably, bat and ball.

Softball

This excellent game has strong parallels with baseball. It uses a larger, softer ball, and is suitable for Key Stages 3 and 4.

- The game is played on a marked diamond-shaped pitch placed in the centre of a larger area, preferably grassed, known as the 'field of play'. This should be at least half the size of a football pitch (*see diagram*).

- There are two types of *Softball*, 'fast pitch' and 'slow pitch', with the dimensions of the pitching and inter-base distance varying both with the type and the age and sex of the players (*see Appendix 2*).

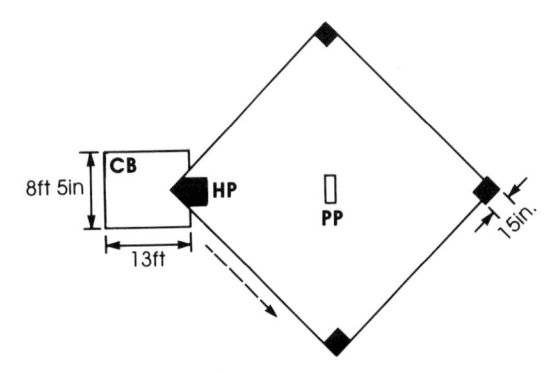

CB = Catcher's box   **HP** = Home plate   **PP** = Pitcher's plate

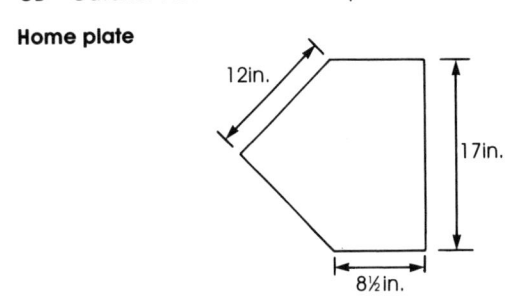

Home plate

- To play the game properly, each base (15 inches square), the pitcher's plate (24 by 6 inches), a home plate and, possibly, a catcher's box should be marked. However, the game can be played quite satisfactorily at class level by using hoops for bases and a simple line or rope or another hoop for pitching, and by giving the catcher free reign.

Striking and Fielding Games

- The area bounded by the four inter-base lines is called the **infield**.
- The **outfield** is the area beyond the **infield**, bounded by imaginary lines running out as continuations of the marked lines linking the home plate to first and third bases.
- The remaining area outside these solid and imaginary lines is **foul territory**.
- The standard team consists of nine (fast pitch) or ten (slow pitch) players. Larger groups can be catered for by allowing more fielders and batters, playing two games in parallel, or dividing a class into three teams with two playing the full game and one playing a solo version or another game.

The full rules and pitch layout for the official version can be obtained from the National Softball Federation (*see Appendix 1*). However, to play a full game at schools level, the following will suffice.

Pitching

1 The pitcher stands with both feet on the plate or behind a line and may only move one foot one step forward in delivering the ball.

2 The ball must be delivered **underhand**, ie released when the hand is still below hip height and the wrist no further from the body than the elbow.

3 The ball when released must pass over the home base at a height no lower than the batter's knee and no higher than the shoulder.

4 Each 'good' ball fulfilling these conditions is called a **strike**; each pitch failing to do so is called a **ball**. If the batter swings at a ball it becomes a strike.

Hitting

5 The batter is allowed three attempts at or hits on good balls.

6 The ball may land in the infield or outfield but not in foul territory (a hit that bounces in the infield and then goes into foul territory is also a foul ball).

Scoring and running

7 One run is scored by each player who successfully negotiates all the bases to finish at the home plate.

8 Progress between bases is made

- by the ball being hit legally forward and with all players currently on bases being able to run
- through 'stealing' – that is, aiming to make the next base on a strike on which the batter does not run (this cannot be done while the ball is in the pitcher's hand).
- as a result of errors by the fielding team: four balls (ie foul pitches) called by the umpire, the final (third) strike dropped by the catcher, or if the batter is struck by the ball when not attempting to strike it – in these cases the batter is allowed to walk to the first base and as two players are not allowed on one base at the same time, any occupant is allowed to move on and similarly at any subsequent base.

Getting out

9 A batter is out
   - if **any** hit is caught by a fielder
   - after missing three fair balls (called 'struck out'), providing the ball is caught by the catcher
   - if first base, or any subsequent base to which a runner is forced to run because all behind are occupied and the batter elects to run, is touched with any body part by a fielder holding the ball before the incoming runner arrives – this is called 'forced-out'
   - if after a fair hit he/she is tagged-out, ie touched by the ball or hand of a fielder holding the ball, while running to a base when not forced to do so, or when leaving the base before the ball is delivered
   - if when a catch is made any runners having left their bases fail to return before the baseman, in contact with the base, receives the ball.

Players are allowed to over-run first base and return without penalty but in the case of second and third bases must maintain contact or they are liable to be run out.

Game basis

10 An innings is completed when three players are out, the next batter in line becoming the first in the next innings, and so on.

11 Each match can consist of a number of innings, with seven being played in the authorised form.

Fast and slow pitch
There are some differences in the rules.

Pitching

Fast pitch The ball is delivered (underarm) with a 'whiplash windmill' action that produces a fast and flat ball.

Striking and Fielding Games

Slow pitch The ball is again delivered underarm but using a lob through an arc of 2–4 metres.

Stealing

Fast pitch A runner may move as the ball is being released and before the ball is struck.

Slow pitch Runners must maintain contact with the base until the ball is actually hit.

'Bunting' – tapping the ball into the infield without really swinging the bat. This is legal in *Fast pitch* but not in *Slow pitch*.

Foul territory

Slow pitch A batter who hits the third strike into foul territory is automatically out.

Fast pitch This is not the case unless the ball is caught.

- The only equipment required to play the game at a basic level is a softball bat, a softball ball, and a pair of catcher's gloves. If the ball is being propelled at high speeds, protective clothing should be worn by the batters and catchers.

- In order to improve the skills required in the game, special practices may be required using the softball bat, ball, etc. As for *Stoolball*, most of the basic and scoring practices listed in Unit 1 could be adopted, with some adaptation of distances, marker siting, etc and with the necessary stress on the specialist techniques made.

- Many of the rounders-type games could be played using a softball bat and ball either on the diamond or using the modified courts as described in Unit 1 (eg *Passball, Tunnelball, Archball, Danish rounders*).

Minor games

Driveball
An interesting variation on the idea of hitting/driving a ball forward and scoring runs is to use a netball court, or a similar shape marked on grass – *see diagram*.

- The game is normally played with two equal teams (6–10 players) but, as with many of the activities described in previous units, it may be adapted for play on a solo basis.

- The game can be based on rounders-type hitting or cricket batting (with or without stumps).

1 The striker **S** stands behind the base line with the wicket-keeper or backstop **W** behind.

Longball, softball, stoolball and minor games

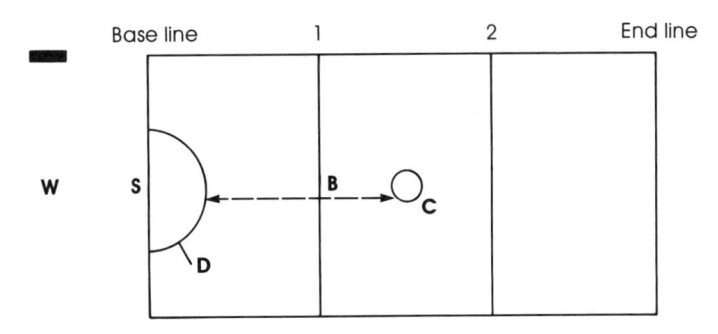

```
        Base line      1           2       End line
        ┌──────────────┬───────────┬──────────┐
        │              │           │          │
  W   S │  )───────────┼─→ B  ○    │          │
        │  D/          │       C   │          │
        │              │           │          │
        └──────────────┴───────────┴──────────┘
```

W = Wicket-keeper or backstop   S = Striker   B = Bowler
D = Marked semicircle at the end of a netball court   C = Centre circle
←− − −→ Running line

2 The bowler **B** stands behind the first line and must deliver with both feet behind it.

3 Each striker receives one 'over' of deliveries consisting of from four to six balls, depending on time, etc.

4 Rounders-type bowling may be used, or an underarm cricket lob to bounce just in front of the striker and encourage driving, although some form of overarm bowling could be used if desired, with the necessary adjustment of distances.

5 The object is to hit/drive the ball forward of the base line and to score as many runs as possible on each strike by running between the semi-circular D in front of the base line and the centre circle.

6 A player completing his/her runs in the centre is allowed to walk back.

7 From strikes that bounce initially within the confines of the netball court, two runs are scored for each 'trip' between the D and the circle. For balls that clear the lines or are touched before bouncing, just one run is scored for each journey.

8 The hitter is out if he/she is
   - caught
   - run out by a player receiving the ball with at least one whole foot in either the D or the circle before the runner is 'home'
   - touched by a player holding the ball
   - if stumps are being used as in cricket, the ball when bowled hits the wicket.

9 No runs may be scored if the ball is hit behind or missed.

10 A player may be out, as in real cricket or rounders, or may start with a credited score and have runs deducted for each time caught, run out, etc (*see Units 1 and 4*), and receive all the balls allowed in the over.

Striking and Fielding Games

Hitting hoop ball
This game, again suited to both rounders or cricket striking, is designed for basically seven a side with, say, two games taking place in any one class.

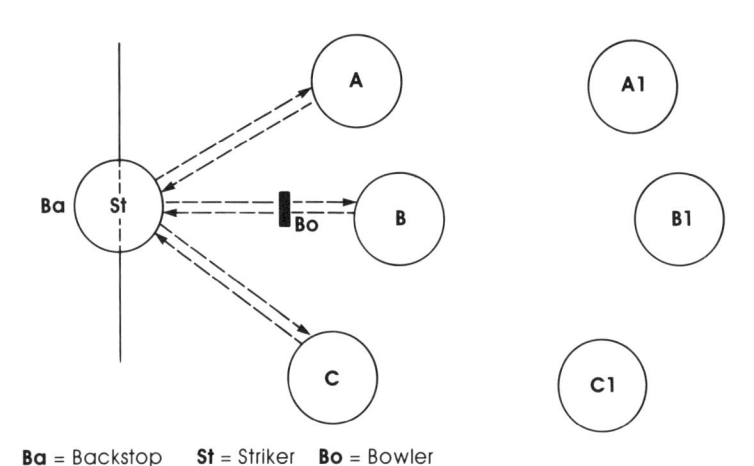

Ba = Backstop   **St** = Striker   **Bo** = Bowler
---▶ Running lines
A, A1, B, B1, C and **C1** are fielders standing in hoops.
The striker (**St**) stands in a hoop when using a rounders bat.

1 The bowler, who is drawn from the batting team, bowls three consecutive balls to the striker on demand.

2 All the balls must be hit forwards and, possibly, be restricted to passing between hoops **A** and **C**.

3 The first ball struck must be fielded by the fielder standing in hoop **A1** and returned to the fielder standing in hoop **A**, the second by **B1** returned to **B** and the third by **C1** returned to **C**. **A**, **B** and **C** must each be holding a ball and in the correct circle before the hitter has to stop running.

4 Any balls missed by the striker are fielded by the backstop and returned to the appropriate hoop.

5 While a fielder is retrieving and returning the ball, the hitter is attempting to run to hoop **A** and back to the base hoop, to hoop **B** and back and, finally, to **C** and back, scoring a run for each 'trip' up to a maximum of six.

6 Hitters are out to catches and if they are still running between hoops when the 'last' ball is secured by a fielder in a hoop.

7 Fielders may be changed round, say after three hitters have had their turns, either by reversing each pair or by moving pairs to different hoops and/or changing the backstop.

Longball, softball, stoolball and minor games

- An excellent feature of this game is that the bowler is a member of the batting team and will therefore aim to ensure that 'good' balls are bowled and when the hitter wants them. The contest is therefore one of good batting against good fielding.

- As in the majority of games, the distances and in this case the angles between the home base and hoops **A** and **C** can be set to cater for cricket or rounders and for different ages and ability levels.

- For cricket the base hoop may be dispensed with and the running done to a line.

- More fielding activity can be brought into the game by
  - having the collector throw to the next in line of the end hoops and then on to the inner hoop (eg **A1** fields and throws to **B1** who throws to **B**, if **B1** fields, to **C1** and **C**, etc)
  - on collection by one fielder the ball being thrown on to all the remaining five fielders in the hoops, with distances set accordingly.

Whole team longball

Two teams of, ideally, 7–10 players play the game on a rectangular court.

1. The width can be any measure above a minimum of 15 metres and the length can vary according to the speed and power of the players (for example, a full gymnasium length can be used when played indoors at secondary level).

2. All players in one team line up behind the base line, one player being the striker with a bat.

3. The striker on being bowled a normal ball with a tennis ball aims to hit it as far as possible forward, and remains behind the line.

4. As soon as contact is made, the remaining players on the batting team try to reach the end line before the ball is returned to the bowler who must have one or both feet, as decided, inside the bowling square or hoop. All who do so receive one point.

5. Additionally, players who have gained the end line may attempt to return to the base line – obviously a difficult thing to do. If they succeed they receive three, four or five points according to perceived difficulty **but** if they fail they forfeit the one point gained for reaching the end line.

6. All players in the batting team have one hit each before the

Striking and Fielding Games

teams change over and one or more innings can be played.

- As in *Multiball rounders*, more than one ball may be used.

- The striker may hit three or more balls in order to involve more fielders or to match the difficulty to a given marked area to be used, such as a netball court.

- When it is deemed to be safe, the fitness element can be emphasised more by runners having to cross benches placed in lines across the court, by jumping over, stepping on or touching with hands.

Unit 6 Making up practices and games

The National Curriculum stresses that children, with an adequate foundation, should be given the opportunity to invent their own practices and games. Groupwork, in units of as low as two but normally three to six pupils, provides an ideal framework for this, with either all the pupils working on making up a game, or just one group doing so while the rest of the class work on different forms of practice.

The object may be to produce

- a simple practice, possibly with scoring, or a relay involving rolling, throwing, bouncing or catching or, later, hitting and bowling

- a game suitable for playing either with equal sides or as a solo or pairs game
    – for the numbers actually in the group
    – for larger teams, the whole class, etc.

It is important to note that the equipment given to a group for inventing a game will in itself act as a catalyst for certain ideas.

- If necessary, limitations may be imposed to stop pupils trying to adhere too closely to forms of game that might be suggested by particular types of equipment. For example, a game must be produced using a cricket bat that does **not** allow runs to be scored in the conventional manner up and down a pitch, or vice versa with a rounders or softball bat where runs **must** be scored in this way.

- Both the number and form of the items of equipment will serve to shape what is possible, particularly the type and size of the hitting implement (if used) and the ball. For example, two hoops (with, say, one bat – padder, rounders, stoolball or cricket) may be expected to produce a different game from one using six cones, marker domes, etc, or if two of each kind of bat had been allowed.

- Groups of different sizes can work with the same equipment and come up with quite different results for the different-sized groups.

- To ensure that copying is reduced or eliminated, one group only may be set to work on inventing a game or practice while the rest work on prescribed activities. Alternatively each group may work with different equipment, spaces, etc. The product may be recorded for future use by the whole class.

The teacher's role

The teacher's role is, through questioning and discussion, to stimulate ideas and, where necessary, help the pupils make their own changes in form, scoring modes, rules and distances so that an activity becomes viable or is improved and may be tried by the rest of the class. It is **not** the role of the teacher to **tell** pupils what is best.

Pupils' roles

- It can be very helpful if one pupil in each group is 'put in charge', acting as a filter for ideas, encouraging each group member to make a contribution, deciding what should be tried out initially and what changes, in the light of observation and, normally, discussion/suggestion should be made in respect of game or practice structure and rules.

- Groups can be made up of pupils of like ability or like personality, so that hopefully the majority will be confident enough to undertake the role of leader and will benefit from the opportunity to take on responsibility (discussions, decision making, etc).

- Different pupils can take on the role of 'leader', either while working on the same practice/game or when the exercise is repeated with a different set of equipment and/or limitations.

- All pupils should benefit from the experience, particularly with good teacher guidance, in respect of learning about, for example, what makes a game viable, and the nature and need for rules.

Making up practices and games is best attempted only when pupils have achieved sufficiently high performance levels in the skills that may be employed in the games/practices, and have some experience of playing in games themselves, particularly those involving the same sort of numbers as are in the group.

Equipment that could be used

For fielding practices or relays

1, 2, 4 or 6 tennis, rounders or cricket balls, with

- 2 or 4 skipping ropes
- 1, 2, 3, 4 hoops
- 2, 4 or 6 cones, marker domes or rounders bases
- 1 or 2 sets of cricket stumps
- combinations of the above, eg 1 hoop and 2 bases or sets of stumps.

2, 4 or 6 beanbags may be used instead of the balls to promote throwing and catching as opposed to rolling, and to make it easier for poorer performers.

2 quoits may also be used as a difficult alternative.

For batting/bowling practices or games

1 rubber or tennis or rounders/cricket ball as appropriate, with 1 or 2 padder or rounders or stoolball or cricket bats, with, for example,

- 2, 3, 4 or 6 hoops
- 2, 4 or 6 cones
- 2 hoops and 1 or 3 cones/bases
- 1 cone and 4 hoops
- 2 sets of stumps and 2 cones and/or 2 hoops.

If a multiball-type activity is envisaged, two or more small balls or larger balls – without bats – may be used occasionally for variety.

Airflow balls can be useful, particularly in restricted space.

More padder/rounders bats, etc can be allowed if each player is to carry the bat round a base circuit as part of the game.

Unit 7 Lesson form, organisation and safety

Lesson form

1 In the later stages of Key Stage 1 and the early stages of Key Stage 2, basic throwing, catching, rolling and picking-up activities may be practised by the whole class in pairs or occasionally in groups. A whole lesson may be spent on these practices or they may be integrated with other activities, particularly those using the same or other small apparatus (*see Appendix 1*).

2 Following the grounding in fielding, basic bowling and batting practices are introduced.
   - These activities may be done in pairs but more often – where, say, the ball passes through a hoop or is hit past the bowler or a backstop is used – such activities will be based on groups of three or four.
   - They may, rarely, be practised throughout a whole lesson, but more usually are integrated **either** with fielding work **or** with different aspects of groupwork (*see Appendix 1*) consecutively and/or in parallel.

3 When pupils move on to working on practices that positively stress more than one skill, are competitive, etc they may start the lesson with revision of simpler work, probably in smaller units, before moving on to work in groups. The groupwork may, in the early part of Key Stage 2,
   - involve all the pupils working on the same practices
   - be based on moving round a 'circuit' of different activities
   - less often, be integrated with other types of ball skill work.

4 To cater for different potential and rates of progress, pupils, working in ability groups, possibly varying in size from pairs upwards, will soon need differentiated activities with **either**
   - all the groups working on the same practice (at different skill levels) **or**
   - some or all working on different activities in parallel, possibly for different time spans.

The groups

- will attempt the type of practice described in Unit 2
- may occasionally undertake activities specifically for assessment

- should, when sufficiently experienced, attempt making-up activities either with just one or all groups involved
- may, possibly, for interest, occasionally attempt proficiency award scheme tests (*see Appendix 3*).

5 As soon as a given basic skill has been established, the children can also begin to play the games, selected from Units 3 to 5, which allow that particular skill to be developed and are structured to allow plenty of activity for all (eg for just throwing and catching, *Passball rounders* with the ball rolled or thrown out). As more skills develop and to higher levels, more demanding games, matched to ability, will be attempted. These games may be played
- in parallel with practices
- following practices or, sometimes, throughout a whole lesson
- with all playing the same game (possibly more than one match, at different skill levels)
- as skill levels diverge, some playing one game, others other games, possibly incorporating small-side and solo versions.

6 Finally, some opportunity must be given for children to play **the complete game**, or modified versions that are recognised by the pupils as being akin to the 'real' thing, but which allow more participation.

Types of lesson: Summary

1 Basic practices, mostly working in pairs, either all based on striking and fielding games skills or integrated with other small apparatus work.

2 All groupwork, working on the same (probably at graded skill levels) or different practices, some or all of which may be competitive.

3 Part basic practices, part groupwork.

4 Part practices (which may be based on groupwork), part games. Groupwork as a part or whole of a lesson may include or be based entirely on making-up games or practices.

5 All small-side games, including scaled-down versions of major games.

6 All solo or pairs versions of games.

7 Games with larger sides, including recognised major varieties.

8 A mixture of different types of games as in **5**, **6** and **7** above.

Striking and Fielding Games

The content of a given lesson would depend largely on the needs of the individual class members as reflected in the progress made within a Key Stage, the balance of material across the sessions devoted to striking/fielding work, the lesson time and total time available, and such factors as facilities and space.

It is vitally important, however, that too much time is not devoted to games *per se*, and that practices, particularly those aligned to the games and which, providing the right help is given at the right time, are the key to developing real **skill**, should form the major part of the work done throughout Key Stage 2 and most of Key Stage 3.

Organisation of pupils

Pairs

Pupils should normally be expected to select their own partners and to sit or crouch when they have done so. This is a simple method that tends to stop children continually changing partners and makes it very easy for both pupils and teacher to see who has not yet got a partner. As children of like ability tend to go together, they are usually well matched in terms of task difficulty.

Groups

In the early stages the most simple method is, again, to allow the pupils to form their own groups either from scratch or by combining pairs.

Another relatively simple method is to have the pupils line up in a double column of pairs:

$$\frac{A1 \quad B1 \quad C1 \quad D1 \quad E1 \quad F1 \quad G1 \quad H1 \quad I1}{A2 \quad B2 \quad C2 \quad D2 \quad E2 \quad F2 \quad G2 \quad H2 \quad I2}, etc$$

As more skilful and confident pupils tend to come to the front, it is simple to split off the requisite number of pairs to form groups all the way down the line (eg **A1**, **A2**, **B1**, **B2** to form one group of four), with a very good chance of achieving matched ability. Some changes may be made either immediately or in the light of responses to practices.

As the pupils progress, the teacher will normally deliberately select groups, possibly varying in size according to ability and need and the type of activity, and depending on whether some sort of balance is wanted, eg between the sexes, or if certain pupils are to be kept apart.

Teams

For games

Selecting teams of equal ability to play each other has long been a problem in games lessons. The most efficient way in terms of both matching and speed is to have the class line up in a double column of matched pairs (*see above*). The teacher splits the line at a given point, depending on how many are required in a team. For example, **A1, B1, C1, D1, E1** and **F1** would play **A2, B2, C2, D2, E2** and **F2** in a six-a-side game.

The better players therefore play together and all can be expected to play a full part. This is something that may not happen if poorer class members are included with better players and are outclassed. Similarly average and weaker players play in matched groups and have better opportunities of expressing themselves within the game. If just two complete teams are needed then one column becomes one team and plays the other column.

Similarly, if, as suggested for some of the games, a class of, say 25–36 is to be divided into three units of equal strength, with two teams playing each other and the third either playing a solo-based or small-sided game or doing one or more practices before playing the winner, or loser, from the first two teams, ask the children to get into threes and then to line up in three lines with each set of three abreast.

One method of obtaining teams should **never** be used: that of pupils acting as captains and picking the remaining class members in turn. Not only does it often lead to imbalanced teams, but it can be most painful for the less competent – already only too aware of their own shortcomings – who are selected last.

For relays

Although it is very difficult to produce teams of three or four of exactly equal ability, it is vital that the attempt is made. Random picking or pupil self-selection does not work and the teacher must attempt to balance good, average and poor in each team and to make changes if necessary to ensure that all have a chance of winning at some point in the session. Team numbers should be kept as small as is possible for a given activity.

Setting up practices and games

1. Pupils carry out balls and bats, etc as required, in baskets, bins or bags. If, as in the case of bats, stumps, cones, hoops, etc they are loose, they must be carried in multiples, **never** singly, thus removing the opportunity for pupils to play with them en route.

2 A practice situation or a game is actually set up and demonstrated at the same time as it is described. It is never simply explained without a demonstration.

3 The markers, poles, wickets, etc are carried out and set up in the proper designated space and are checked before the activity begins. Adequate space **must** be left between practices or games – this may vary from as little as 2–3 metres to as much as 40 metres in the case of certain hard ball activities.

4 More activities can take place in limited areas through the use of modified games and practices using airflow/gamester or sponge balls.

5 For groupwork, where different sets of pupils are working on different activities in parallel, all groups are told what to set up, and precisely where, before they are allowed to collect any equipment. The teacher checks for correct layout and inter-group spacing before the practice or game begins, even before balls are distributed.

Safety

Surfaces

All surfaces must be in good condition and free from dangerous objects and should be checked prior to use. There should not be any holes or loose gravel, glass or tins, etc that could cause injury. Gym/sports halls, or school halls with wet floors are extremely dangerous and should never be played on. Sections of wet floor should be cordoned off.

Distances

- All activities must take place a safe distance from windows, walls, portable equipment, etc, and anything that juts out dangerously. Particular care should be taken with any activity that involves hard running or a hard ball.

- Activities should not be sited so that there is any danger of balls (particularly hard ones) being hit onto roads, paths or other public places.

- Adequate distances must be left between certain practices or games being played in parallel, in order to avoid the possibility of a fielder in one game being hit by a hard ball struck in another game, or of collisions between fielders.

Lesson form, organisation and safety

- Games using airflow balls, etc may be played in closer proximity to buildings, and to other games using similar equipment.
- Fielders in all hitting games should stand a sensible distance away from the striker (*see Specific activities, Cricket* below).

Equipment

- All equipment should be checked regularly for wear and tear, for example loose bat handles, splinters on bats, stumps or skittles, split seams on balls, etc.
- Only safe objects should be used as markers: cones, skittles, beanbags, etc – never cricket stumps or chairs.
- Items of equipment no longer in use should not be left lying around within or at the side of a playing area; they are potentially hazardous and can cause nasty falls, sprains, etc. All must be carried and **put away** either in the proper receptacle or at a designated point some distance from the working area. They should **never** simply be rolled or thrown towards the storage area.
- Hitting implements in games such as rounders, longball, etc should normally be carried while running in order to avoid the very real danger of them being thrown and hitting another child rather than put down on a spot. If there is such a shortage of equipment that bats cannot be carried, the children may be required to drop the bat into a container or hoop before the run is made, or while on route to first base.

Kit

Different types of suitable clothing may be worn. It is essential that pupils always wear appropriate footwear (trainers, gym-shoes, etc). Games should not be played in bare feet. On no account should

- ordinary shoes, plastic sandals or spiked running shoes be worn
- indoor work be done in stockinged feet
- any activity be attempted with a cardigan or tracksuit top hanging open, or in dresses or ordinary long trousers
- medallions, badges, earrings, bracelets, watches, rings, etc be worn.

Specific activities

Cricket

When cricket games and practices are played with a hard ball, special precautions have to be taken.

- Protective clothing of the correct size and type must be worn by batters and wicket-keepers. This includes gloves, pads and if bowling is going to be fast, abdominal guards and (in the case of boys) boxes.

- Playing-pitch surfaces, whether grass or artificial, must be flat and free from cracking in order to obtain an even bounce.

- Fielders must not be allowed to stand too near to the bat, particularly on the leg side. The English Schools Cricket Association's general rule states:

  'No fielder in under 14 or 15 games shall be allowed to field nearer than eight yards measured from the middle stump, except behind the wicket on the off side and as wicket-keeper. At under 13 and below the distance shall be eleven yards. A fielder may be allowed to move forward into the restricted area to make a catch or field the ball provided that he/she was outside the area when the stroke was made.'

Simple marks can be used to indicate the restricted area.

Softball

As stated in Unit 5, appropriate protective clothing is necessary when fast pitching is being employed (*see Appendix 1*).

Relays

Pupils must not run to touch a solid object such as a wall as a turning or finishing point in races. They should turn round safe markers such as cones, domes or beanbags, and should finish either by returning to a given point or by crossing a finishing line. There should be sufficient distance, related to the speed being generated, to allow a runner to pull up comfortably before reaching any solid or portable object. Plenty of room (a minimum of 2 metres) should be left between teams competing in parallel.

The teacher

Teachers should

- have full knowledge of all safety points, both of a general nature and, particularly, in respect of the activities covered
- keep checking to see that pupils are working within prescribed/marked limits
- keep checking to see that equipment is being used in the correct way and that none has been left lying in a dangerous position
- know what to do in case of accident.

Further information on safety can be found in the definitive (DES approved) *Safe Practice in Physical Education*, published by BAALPE (the British Association of Advisers and Lecturers in PE). This is available from LEA Physical Education Advisers, or White Line Press, 60 Bradford Road, Stanningley, Leeds LS28 6EF.

Unit 8 Development and assessment

'In order for a pupil to learn, it is necessary for the teacher to provide appropriate learning situations, give guidance and facilitate progression. An effective teacher is continually assessing every individual pupil's attainment and needs, and, as a result, is creating or adapting the learning situation . . . assessment does not inhibit teaching; it is teaching! S. Robinson, 1992

For progress to be made, the teacher must

- establish clear aims that he/she **believes** in
- provide appropriate and properly tiered learning experiences to satisfy the aims and, finally,
- utilise assessment procedures which will clearly show to what degree they have been realised.

The broad aims can be based on the End of Key Stage Statements in the National Curriculum, with more detailed objectives, linked to the specific Programmes of Study, being dovetailed with the learning experiences provided within each aspect. Where possible, criteria, linked to assessable outcomes, should be established for measuring the degree of progress achieved in any one area, criteria which as far as possible are understood by the pupils. The outcomes, linked to activities, increasing in respect of difficulty or the demands made on an individual/group, should allow for the measurement and recording of ongoing attainment to be made.

The assessment process – broadly the gathering of evidence on the effects of teaching a given programme, ideally through its effects on each child – never determines what is taught. Neither is it an 'independent' element which may or may not be tacked-on at given end-points of subject aspect blocks. It is an ongoing integral part of the learning process, providing the essential feedback which enables evaluation of

a what individual progress has been made by both staff **and** pupils (and hence in turn aiding motivation)

b the effectiveness of the material used and the way in which it has been presented

c vitally, the future needs of **all** the pupils.

If group and individual progress is not continually assessed then material cannot be matched to the varying needs and will, as often in the past, be of a 'hit and miss' nature, aimed en masse and suiting only a number of the pupils in a class or group.

The aims in striking/fielding work, as in all games, may be quite wide, embracing, for example,

- the need for plenty of activity
- the improvement of skill
- the ability to observe accurately, analyse, etc, appreciate and comment on strengths and weaknesses of opponents and self
- interpretation, problem solving, decision making, tactics
- knowledge of safety and/or rules
- the ability to work with others
- the less tangible, but to many vital though difficult to assess, 'personal' elements such as enthusiasm or perseverance, or maintaining a 'sporting' attitude at all times.

Although accepting that reference may be made to any of these in reports, etc, in practice it is necessary, given the time constraints, to limit what is to be measured. All teachers in Key Stages 2 and 3 will be positively interested in developing, assessing and evaluating **performance** and **understanding.**

Acquisition of a technique or isolated skill

These 'closed' skills are developed and may be demonstrated outside the game situation. They cover the whole range of fielding (including picking up, catching and throwing) and striking skills.

Catching development, for example, requires a large range of different practices using different balls, at different distances, projected with different forces, at different heights, static and moving at different speeds over different distances, two hands and one – preferred or not – and under different pressures in regard to returning. The outcomes that can be assessed are the same as the practices and are, therefore, virtually unlimited. Those selected to measure progress in Key Stages 2 and 3 could include, for example,

- catching a ball thrown
  - from 5 metres away, parallel to the ground at stomach height
  - in an arc of 45° or more at a minimum distance of 30 metres
  - between knee and ground to be caught one-handed 2–3 metres to one side of the starting position

- hitting or driving a ball
  - forwards from an 'easy' delivery
  - over or between two posts placed at given angles and/or distances.

The assessment could be made in several different ways.

- As a 'one-off': does the child succeed in catching, hitting the ball, etc on one attempt? This has the virtue of simplicity and is time saving. It tells us little, however, about consistency or how well the action was carried out.
- Based on three, six or ten attempts, giving more information on **how often** a child is successful.
- Based partially on objective target success (eg whether the ball is caught and, possibly, how often) and also on the **quality** of execution, the positioning of the feet, the balance, the movement of the arms, the pathway and final position of the bat, etc.

Giving graded marks out of ten or using a simple three-point system can give a reasonably accurate current picture.

Example Catching a ball thrown high, on the move

3 points Catches it 90–100% and/or moves confidently into correct feet position 'under' the ball. Holds easily, pulls in, maintains balance throughout.

2 points Catches it 50–90%, keeps eye on ball but is not always right under it. Normally takes up good position, may snatch, does not always bring it in immediately. Sometimes a little unbalanced.

1 point Catches it 20–50%. Some difficulty in following flight, sometimes positioned correctly (particularly feet), but sometimes unbalanced, holds if hands close on ball, often snatches or holds arms rigid.

Pupils with 3 points are very competent and need more demanding work: covering bigger distances, balls thrown higher or flatter with more power, one-handed, etc.

Pupils with 2 points will benefit from some more practice at the tested skill with some alternative work: lower arcs, running forward and sideways to take. Some stress is needed on the aspects of the technique that are not always done well.

Pupils attaining only 1 point need to work systematically, in turn, on facets of the technique, mostly using simpler throws: lower height or angle, shorter distance to move, etc. Some of these in the last group, and those who were not good enough to attempt the test, may work on simpler, more static or limited movement practices.

Using a multi-attempt approach can be very time-consuming, particularly if done by the teacher. However, this is an ideal situation for the children to be involved in, normally in twos, sometimes in threes. The pupils can count and record their own or their partner's scores. In the latter part of Key Stage 2 particularly, and throughout Key Stage 3, they can 'mark' technical ability, either by checking against one to three points listed by the teacher, or by using a self-devised set of criteria. Feedback can also be given to the performer, helping to improve his/her skill. Detailed observation of this sort adds to purpose and interest and, in improving understanding of the technique, often leads to improvement of the observer's own actions. The pupils can record the results by ticks or numbers, or even comments, in rough or directly onto class or personal profile sheets. A class techniques recording chart can be designed as follows.

	Skills			
Name	A	B	C	
	0 1 2 3	0 1 2 3	0 1 2 3	
Black, W.	✓			
Brown, F.	✓			
Green, H.	✓ •			
Grey, M.	•			
Rose, A.	✓			
White, G.	✓ •			

| Date (1) ✓ | 5.5.94 |
| Date (2) • | 7.7.94 |

A key can show which 'skill' is represented by each letter (for example, A: catching a ball, thrown towards the chest with moderate pace from a distance of 5 metres, with two hands, while in a static position; C: catching a ball thrown high, while on the move). Different colours or symbols can be used to show at a glance when a given standard was achieved (that is 1, 2 or 3, or 0 if the first standard was not reached). Duplicated sheets can be used for the whole school, with blanks for names, class, PE aspect and dates to be filled in.

Charts of this sort may help to show what aspects need special attention when working on a technique. When they are used in combination with practice designed to improve a score, work on positive aspects of a technique or, in the case of the very successful, making increased demands, such charts can clearly be very productive.

Such technique charts, showing both the current state and past progress of the class at a glance, is of great value to a teacher. It is a great advantage too to both teacher and pupil for each child to develop a personal portfolio of achievements and information. The pupil can follow his/her own progress and can start with double-column 'strips' for profiles in each PE aspect.

Example

NAME	CLASS	DATE

Striking and Fielding	0	1	2	3
1 Pick up rolling ball, throw underhand to base or stumps					....
2 Run and throw to fielder in hoop					....
3 Hit ball with bat through posts directly in front (may use prescribed shot in cricket)					....

Space may be left for written comments.

'Open' or applied skill

Tests of the sort described above, tracing the progression of technique development, are easily administered, and allow scope for pupil observation, comment, etc. In allowing progress to be so clearly shown, they can be very motivating. They do have some value in showing improvement in 'skill', but they also have serious limitations in that they do not provide evidence of ability to actually **play** a game.

> *'A "good" games player is not one who can perform skills in isolation, but one who can apply them appropriately and effectively within the game situation.'*
>
> Berks TVI, *Physical Education – Assessment in Perspective*

Some of the techniques practised 'in isolation' are fortunately replicated in an almost identical way within striking games, eg taking a catch from a high hit or hitting a ball bowled in the same way as in practice. However, these 'closed' skills played in an 'open' situation are subject to different pressures. For example:

- The ball dropped in practice does not affect the rest of the class; in the open situation it means a lost 'life' or a score to the opposition, creating psychological pressure for the pupil aiming to catch the ball.

- A ball fielded may have to be returned under time pressure, and choices may have to be made (for example, which base or wicket to throw to).

'Skill' means **application within a game**, and its development must, therefore, embrace the learning of techniques on their own, followed by their placing in practices (*see Unit 2*), which aim to replicate game situations and gradually increase pressure through competition (eg with players aiming to get others out) and scoring, increasing numbers etc, allowing gradual progression and more opportunities to practise at their own level. Similarly, playing scaled-down or made-up small-side games allows 'real' practice of skills but, again, with more opportunities to bat/bowl, etc and with less pressure than in a full game.

Progress, again, must be evaluated. Although statistical evidence of batting and bowling, particularly in cricket-type games, may be taken into account, some kind of subjective assessment is needed to show how the pupils respond in a range of situations. Actual comments may be written for each pupil – at, say, the end of a block spent on striking games, or a term – taking into account the progress made against listed criteria and ability at the start. Specific observation of an individual in a game or practice may be done occasionally, possibly using a grading system of, say, A–E, based on prepared statements. The statements, geared to a Key Stage, or a phase within it, may refer to fielding, batting, etc separately, or cover all aspects together.

Example

- A Bats with confidence and accuracy in all practices and games played. Picks up cleanly, returns quickly and reasonably accurately.

- D Can hit the ball in some situations but not always accurately, and may be prone to over-cautiousness or conversely, wildness. Often caught. Picks up reasonably at times, judgement sometimes awry. Can throw accurately to target if not always quickly.

It must not be assumed that a 'good' performer necessarily understands the game and would make a good captain or 'coach', or that a poor performer has not grasped any concepts. Some of the pupils with limited physical attributes, co-ordinations, etc may welcome the opportunity to show that they have **understanding**; that is, they appreciate what is needed in a given game or coaching situation.

The understanding may range from an appreciation of how a technique is done (or why it is used), through choosing an appropriate strike to a given bowl, when to run, etc, taking into account the relative abilities of batting partners or players on bases ahead, how to place fielders and/or what sort of bowling to use in a practice or game to get an individual out or contain runs or rounders.

At some point in Key Stage 3, each pupil must have the opportunity to act as 'captain' and officiate in either a modified or full game. The teacher creates opportunities and ensures that individuals are given the confidence and opportunity to express opinions, relate to other pupils, and are not overawed or 'shouted down' by stronger personalities/better performers. The discussion that may take place can be used as part of the assessment process, as can questioning on a one to one, pairs or group basis. Other assessment 'modes' are based on

- questionnaires
- observation while 'coaching' is taking place
- the pupils recording their own impressions of, for example, techniques observed, or how they may have improved the defence tactics used in a game that had been played.

Notes made by the teacher should be recorded on an individual 'understanding/invention' sheet covering all games work, including making up games, and which could be used as part of the basis for an End of Key Stage PE report.

It is, of course, impossible for the teacher to attempt to question all pupils, make notes, etc each time they are 'coaching' partners or involved in making up a game, or even when a period of time is given over to assessment in this form.

As SEAC states:

> *'It is not necessary to attempt to collect evidence of everything a pupil attains, but rather **to be able to point to key examples of achievement that support particular judgements.**'*

The correct selection of what to assess and what to record is what matters.

Lesson and teaching evaluation

The most important element in ensuring pupil progress is the teacher. The teacher selects, organises and delivers the material and should aim to evaluate his/her 'performance' either continuously and/or in selected lessons or at specific points (eg a block of lessons on striking and fielding). The aspects that may be covered, possibly using some sort of checklist with ticks and/or comments, are as follows.

Material

Suitability according to group/individual need; balance within and across lessons; practice length and repetition. (Did they always have sufficient time for guided practice?)

Organisation

Grouping, pairing, etc according to need is vital; equipment distribution; the setting-up of practices and games.

Communication/development

Personal – voice, positioning, etc; explanations; comments, including the essential **feedback** – to individuals, groups, class – when activities are stopped and while the pupils are working; question and answer; demonstrations; degree of encouragement, praise, with reasons ('reinforcement') – in particular the vital recognition of each individual's progress; individual coaching.

Teaching strategies

Direct – whole class; groups – different levels, problem solving; pupil instruction – in pairs, groups; pupil assessment – self, others, etc.

Overall

- Do the children always appreciate the criteria for success?
- Was sufficient stress laid on the 'right' elements in a practice, and was the demand such that there was actual improvement?
- If improvement was not made, why not, and what is required?
- Are all pupils properly involved in assessment and able to show evidence of attainment?

Summary

Assessment of striking/fielding work should

- help determine pupils' performance levels, knowledge and understanding
- enable recognition of a wide range of achievement to be given
- identify pupils' future needs
- allow improvements to be made in
  - task selection and order of use
  - use of teaching strategies and skills
- provide essential information for departments and teachers who will take the pupils in future – and who **must** use the same kind of graduated 'steps' for progression and apply and fully understand the meaning of the same criteria in assessment/evaluation.

Appendix 1 *Useful sources of information*

Further information on basic practices in hitting, throwing/catching, rolling, etc and relays plus teaching and assessment, may be obtained from:

J. Severs, *Activities for PE Using Small Apparatus*, Stanley Thornes (Publishers) Ltd.

Further information on some basic techniques and practices may be obtained from:

A. Cooper, *The Development of Games and Athletics Skills*, Stanley Thornes (Publishers) Ltd.

Detailed information on assessment is available in:

S. Robinson, *Assessment in Physical Education – a Development Programme*, BAALPE, 1992.
Obtainable from Studies in Education Ltd, Driffield Road, Nafferton, Driffield, East Yorkshire YO25 0JL.

Information on rules, markings, equipment and coaching publications may be obtained from national governing bodies:

Cricket The Cricket Council, Lord's, London NW8 8QZ. Kwik cricket – game and skills award.
Tel. 071-289 2419. Competitions.

National Cricket Association (Coaching Section), Edgbaston, Birmingham. Tel. 021-440 1748.

English Schools Cricket Association (Competitions), 38 Mill House, Woods Lane, Cottingham, Hull HU16 4HQ.

Rounders National Rounders Association, 3 Denehurst Avenue, Nottingham NG8 5DA Tel. 0602 785514.

Softball National Softball Federation, PO Box 1303, London NW3 5TU.

Stoolball National Stoolball Association, Sales Officer, 18 Victory Road, Horsham, West Sussex.

Appendix 2 *Dimensions and equipment sizes*

Information is given where different court/pitch dimensions and/or equipment sizes are recommended for pupils of different ages, sex or, occasionally, size.

Cricket

Recommendations by the National Cricket Association are for both boys and girls. Ages are linked to a starting date at the beginning of the school year (September).

Pitch

Under 9	17 yards
Under 10	18 yards
Under 11	19 yards
Under 12	20 yards
Under 13	21 yards
Under 14 and above	22 yards

Stumps

All ages up to and including
Under 13	27 x 8 in. (68 x 20 cm)
Under 14 and above	27 x 9 in. (68 x 23 cm)

Ball

When a hard cricket-type ball is used:
Under 14	4¾ ounces (135 g)
Over 14	5½ ounces (156 g) full size

Bats

Ideally there should be a range of sizes available to cater for the varying heights of the pupils in a given class, group or team. These should range from size 3 for the smallest players at the bottom end of Key Stage 2 up to Harrow and even full size at the top end of Key Stage 3. Care should be taken to ensure that bats which are too heavy are not used.

Run-up

Up to 16 A limit of 15 yards is recommended.

Fielding For minimum recommended distances, *see Unit 7*.

Softball

	Distance	Fast pitch Base (ft)	Fast pitch Pitching (ft)	Slow pitch Base (ft)	Slow pitch Pitching (ft)
Under 11	Girls/boys	55	35	55	35
Under 13	Girls	60	35	60	40
	Boys	60	40	60	40
Under 16	Girls	60	40	65	46
	Boys	60	46	60	46
Under 19	Girls	60	40	65	50
	Boys	60	46	65	50

Appendix 3 *Proficiency awards*

Many sports have awards schemes in which a given achievement level in a series of tests is rewarded with a certificate matched in colour or number to the appropriate grade. Usually pupils have an opportunity to buy a corresponding badge.

These awards may be as simple as the Kwik Cricket Skills Award which has just five tests, covering the following skill areas:

- fielding (catching a lobbed ball at a close distance and picking up a stationary ball and propelling it between two stumps)

- bowling (overarm to bounce and pass through the gap between two posts)

- batting (hitting a ball from a vertical bounce forwards between two stumps and hitting or 'pulling' a lobbed full toss between two stumps placed at right-angles to the line of delivery, ie towards square leg).

More complex awards, like the 'Test' cricket awards demand a certain level of expertise in throwing, retrieving, running, batting, bowling and wicket-keeping. Tests are supplemented by oral questions on cricket teams and players, the laws and basic tactics.

The National Rounders Association has award schemes for children working at Key Stages 2 and 3, with badges and certificates available for each level attained.

However, it is quite easy for a school or group of schools in a district or county to design their own tests, with either a simple pass/fail system for each level of certificate, or an award of different grades according to the scores achieved on all the tests. In the latter case each test must be designed to allow for a wide range of scores to be achieved. Such tests could include the following:

- throwing for distance

- throwing for accuracy (eg to hit a target at different distances, or concentric circles on a wall or on the ground, or to pass on the full or bounce through posts)

- picking up and returning accurately or with speed (eg six balls rolled from a given distance, picked up and thrown back)

Striking and Fielding Games

- rolling for accuracy and/or speed
- batting to hit at different angles for accuracy and/or length (and in the case of cricket different types of delivery)
- bowling for accuracy
- catching balls thrown from different distances and angles
- possibly more specific game skills, such as wicket-keeping, base fielding
- laws of the game, etc.

The testing for such awards may be done by pupils and teachers as an extra-curricular activity or in lessons as groupwork with all or some of the activities based on the award(s) (*see Unit 7*).

Information is available as follows:

Kwik cricket	The Cricket Council, Lord's, London NW 8QZ Tel. 071-289 2419.
'Test' cricket	NCA Proficiency Awards Scheme, Lancashire County Cricket Ground, Old Trafford, Manchester M16 0PX.
Rounders	Mr D. Dorrell, 79 Fernside Road, Poole, Dorset BH15 2JL.